The
Is King:
Keswick 1979

Ec 143 [illegible]
146 [illegible]

The Lord Is King: Keswick 1979

Alec Motyer,
Eric Alexander,
George Duncan,
Oswald Sanders
& others

Edited by David Porter

STL Books
P.O. Box 48, Bromley, Kent, England

Keswick Convention Council, England

STL Books are published by Send The Light Trust,
9 London Road, Bromley, Kent, England.

ISBN 0 903843 20 X

Cover photograph by Canon K. W. Coates.

Made and printed by
Hunt Barnard Printing Ltd., Aylesbury, Bucks.

CONTENTS

INTRODUCTION

by Canon A. S. Neech (Chairman of the Keswick Convention Council)

For more than a hundred years Keswick in Cumbria, England, has drawn crowds of people from all over the world. They come to the two weeks of Convention to hear the Word of God expounded by men of widely different gifts and backgrounds in a huge tent whose platform carries a banner bearing the words from Galatians 3:28, 'All one in Christ Jesus'. Denominational allegiances are forgotten in the essential unity in Christ and in willingness to submit to the teaching and authority of His Word. The hearty singing of over four thousand voices in the tent is itself an inspiration. The quiet beauty of the hills and lakes makes for a restful break from the fret and rush of everyday living. But what people come for, and what takes up nearly all the time allotted for each meeting, except, of course, those called specifically for prayer and the Friday evening Communion Services, is the study of the Scriptures.

In 1979 numbers were as great, if not greater, than in previous years, except the Centenary Year of 1975, and at times a hush that could almost be felt characterised the attention with which they listened. The rustling of the pages of hundreds and hundreds of Bibles as people looked up Scripture references was a memory many carried back to their homes all over the world.

This little book contains fuller reports of the Bible Readings given during both Conventions and abbreviated addresses selected from those given in July 1979. Many readers will be sorry that all the addresses are not included. But space forbids such a lavish spread. Tape recordings were made of all the meetings, and a list of those forming the basis of this book is printed at the end of the book.

May the printed word, with the opportunity it gives for re-reading and reflection, bring blessing to all into whose hands this report now comes. In spoken form God used it to challenge, encourage and guide thousands of His children. When you have read it, pass it on. Keswick's influence is world-wide because of what begins in individual hearts and lives at the Conventions and is then worked out in daily living.

EDITOR'S INTRODUCTION

We drove to Keswick on the opening Sunday, through soft rain which was a welcome change after the weeks of airless heat in the south. No doubt the symbolically-inclined could make something of that. The hills brooded as peacefully as ever in the drizzle. The booths lining the narrow streets near the tents displayed a variety of polythene improvisations; these directed the rain away from assorted Christian literature and down the necks of assorted Christians who took it all in great good humour. It was a constant surprise that so small a town could accommodate so large a gathering; one waited, as if at some evangelical Piccadilly Circus, for everybody one had ever known to pass by and wave a greeting.

A visiting preacher told me once that Keswick during the Convention was as near as you could get to heaven – 'Everybody you see is carrying a Bible!' Despite this commendation it was many years before I got to Keswick, and this year's impressions are very much those of a new boy. It seemed, so far as I could tell, a typical Keswick; mothers sat together with their toddlers, reading Romans and knitting; a speaker's casual joke at the beginning of the week prompted a running controversy in the nicest possible spirit over Bible versions; I picked up a couple of Dorothy L. Sayers detective stories for a shilling in a secondhand bookstall, next to a room packed solid with tea-drinking conventioners; in free time some people went for walks, some went to sleep, others wandered round the town. Being the wrong side of thirty your editor was excluded from the young people's tent, but I am told that motor-cycle impersonations took up at least part of the programme. Everything, I was told, was running very nicely, and the Convention was much as other years.

Impressions, and hasty ones at that. But since Keswick I have had the privilege to work on the tapes and transcripts of the addresses that are reproduced in this book. It is a privilege for two reasons. Firstly, I have had access to all, and heard most, of the talks given at this year's Keswick. A shelf full of cassettes and a pile of transcripts have thus given me an opportunity that few conventioners have had. But secondly, the privilege of editing the material has been a great one. It is a unique experience to read a manuscript word by word, attempting to abbreviate the extent of it while retaining all the subject matter. It concentrates the mind on the message wonderfully, and I have benefited from it enormously. A great many blessings were experienced at Keswick this year, but I don't think anybody else had that particular one, and I'm grateful for it.

Which leads me on to one or two editorial matters. As in previous years, the speakers have not had the opportunity to check the transcripts, and have graciously allowed this material to go to press as it stands. It is however important that the reader should know that what he has in his hands is not a document which has gone through the normal processes of author revisions and double checking that might be expected in a finished book-treatment. It is a transcript of addresses, deliberately edited to retain the flavour of spoken delivery, and not to be seen as the various authors' official, published, finished work. These edited transcripts are intended to reproduce the essence of what was heard from the platform, and should be read in that light.

For that reason, no standardisation of Bible references and versions has been undertaken. Most of the speakers occasionally paraphrased freely the passages they were expounding, and some changed the version they were using according to the point they were making. As you read this book with an open Bible beside you (which is strongly advised) you will notice that the speakers do not always keep exactly to the text. As such paraphrasing was generally very much intentional, no editorial alterations apart from corrections of obvious misreferences and misquotations have been made.

I hope that much of the flavour of the event, and all of the content of the addresses, comes over in these transcripts. Elsewhere in this book you will find a list of tapes available, which contain the full texts of the addresses including asides, illustrations, and some very good jokes, all of which were sacrificed in the interests of making a short and inexpensive book.

I would like to thank the Keswick Convention Council for their support and help in this project, and for reading proofs before publication; the voluntary transcribers who worked on the first set of transcripts soon after Keswick; and Susie Price, who worked at great speed to produce further transcripts from which the final editing was done. All of these and many more have helped to produce this record of the Keswick Convention.

Come to think of it, it probably was a little bit like heaven.

David Porter

THE BIBLE READINGS

A GREAT GOD – A GREAT KING

by Rev. Alec Motyer

1. Psalms 93 and 94: The place of faith, and the place of prayer

We're going to take these two psalms, and we're going to treat them as if they belonged together. I ought therefore to say to you that this is not always a safe way to use the Book of Psalms. It is, like any other hymn book, an anthology; and no more than you would think it significant that hymn 6 followed hymn 5 in any hymn book you might pick up, should you *necessarily* consider it significant that Psalm 94 comes after Psalm 93. But it does seem that Psalms 93 to 100 may have been a little 'hymn book' on their own, put together in a deliberately progressive way. Certainly we can deal with Psalms 93 and 94 as expressing companion truths, each supplementing the other under the one great common theme – the Lord is King.

So let's look at these psalms, first of all in a very general way. Psalm 93 majors on pictures. One of the pictures it gives of this kingly Lord and God is of one whose rule does not go unchallenged. In verse 3 the throne of God is seen as assailed, like a rock by a stormy sea. Psalm 94 speaks of the same truth, not in terms of pictures but of people. In 94:5 we read: 'They break in pieces Thy people, O Lord.' Now this word 'break in pieces' isn't the same one that appears in 93:3, sometimes translated 'pounding waves', but it sounds very like it; and I think that is intended to bind the two psalms together. The Lord's throne is a challenge throne, and the actuality of challenge comes when enemies assail the people of God. Again, 94:2 speaks of an unreal pride, an attempt to usurp God's dignity, contrasting with 93:1 which speaks of the pride that God properly takes in His own nature – His proper and sinless esteem of Himself.

And again, 93:5 affirms the lovely thought of the house of God. 'Holiness becomes Thy house.' There is such a thing as a house of God, and there are therefore members of His household. But it's no more than a truth affirmed. However, when we turn to 94:22, the truth goes beyond affirmation and enters into experience. I hope that these comparisons are showing us how the two psalms balance. Broadly speaking, Psalm 93 deals with affirmation in one way or another and Psalm 94 deals with the experience of the great truths affirmed, down in the arena and conflict where people live. So for example 93:4, 'The Lord on high is mighty' – what a marvellous, compelling statement of the sovereignty of God! Then Psalm 94 speaks of the Lord not as King but as Judge. For example, verse 2, 'Thou Judge of the earth.'

Psalm 93, a King: Psalm 94, a Judge. Psalm 93, His dignity and power: Psalm 94, His executive authority. So the two psalms begin to balance out, as it were, before our very eyes. Now we'll deal with them under the simple headings that arise from those general comparisons.

1. Psalm 93: The King acclaimed

The psalm starts 'The Lord reigneth.' Better, I think, 'The Lord is King.' Do you remember that rough-and-ready chap Jehu, in the Old Testament? Elisha sent one of the sons of the prophet to anoint Jehu as King. He took him into an inner room and anointed him, and afterwards (it's all in 2 Kings 9) his fellow army officers said, 'What did that mad fellow say to you?' When Jehu told them, they took every man his garment and put it under Jehu as a symbol of submission to him. And they sat him on top of the steps and they shouted 'Jehu is King'. Even though the words are reversed in the Hebrew from 2 Kings 9:13 to Psalm 93:1, the thought is the same: 'The Lord is King.' We'll discover Him here.

We discover Him first of all as *the eternal King*. Verses 1, 3 and 4 affirm the present reality of His kingship. Verse 2, however, tells us that this present kingship is not something that suddenly has happened. We stand by the throne and we realise that there has never been a time when it wasn't true that the Lord is King. Verse 5 looks forward – 'for evermore'. So we look forward also and find a King. An eternal King.

Secondly we find one who is *King over this world*. The opening verses of Psalm 93 work downwards – from the Lord, to the world. We're allowed to see the throne and then we're encouraged to let our eyes drop, so we see beneath it the world over which the King reigns. The eye of faith is focusing on the reality of God, and then is open to a living understanding of the reality that is around. The unseen is the ground and explanation of the seen. We are invited in this psalm to draw out the implication: that the created order depends for its stability on the security and the changelessness of a reigning God. Verse 3 depicts the world in all its turbulence, but the result is the same; when we look beyond the reality of the pounding waves we see what the Bible insists is an equal reality – a reigning God. This is a true kingship over the world in which we live.

Thirdly, amplifying 'true kingship', *the Lord is really King*. His kingship is neither idle nor ornamental but real and active. Verse 1 has the metaphor of clothing for this. Joshua, that rather trembling soldier, was given the tough nut to crack of the fortified city of Jericho. So he thought he'd better go and have a look at it, and he went and found himself looking at God. So often that's true, isn't it, of the believer and his problems? He goes to look his problems in the face and finds that God has come to meet him! Well, Joshua 5:13 tells us that the Lord came to him in armour. Why? To show capacity and commitment. 'I *am* able to fight your battles; I *will* fight your battles.' And when the Psalmist says imaginatively, 'Look up, see the God who reigns,' we see that He is wearing the garment. He is a real King! He has the capacity for rule, and He has committed Himself *to* rule. He has absolute power. He really is King.

And fourthly *he is the acknowledged King*. Even though the world is full of turbulence and His reign does not go unchallenged, there are those who acknowledge Him as King. Go back to Jehu. The people shouted out 'Jehu is King,' and they were in effect saying, 'He is sitting on *my* garment. He is *my* King.' God's kingship in the first section of the psalm meets with the response of faith; and in the second section it meets with the response of commitment. Now is the time to share with you the way the two sections hold together. Will you notice, verses 2 and 5 are different from the rest; they are personal addresses made to the great King. Notice verse 2: 'Thou art from everlasting.' Verse 1 stood back: 'The Lord reigneth.' Now verses 3 and 4 go back to this descriptive way. But verse 5 returns to the words of testimony. 'Thy testimonies are very sure.' So the people who say by implication in verse 1 'The Lord is my King,' have certain things they want to say to Him. In verse 2 they say 'Thy throne is established of old: Thou art from everlasting,' and in verse 5 they say 'Thy testimonies are very sure: holiness becometh Thine house, O Lord, for evermore.' So you see, the first section of the psalm starts with the throne and works downwards to the world, and then puts in a little word of testimony. The second section starts with the world, works upwards to the throne, and then puts in a word of testimony. How beautifully put together this psalm is!

What then do the people of God affirm when they acclaim their King? *They endure, as seeing Him who is invisible.* There is an invisible reality, and there is a visible reality. And it is the mark of the people of God that in that situation they identify themselves with the unseen God. Secondly (verse 5), as they testify, *they believe the word which He has vouched for.* Their King has spoken. And they commit themselves to the reality and solidity and reliability of the word which God has spoken and vouched for. And thirdly, *they commit themselves to the holiness which He requires.* It's not explained: 'Holiness becometh Thine house.' The assumption is that it is in the nature of God.

Fifthly, *this reigning God is absolute King.* At no point does Psalm 93 descend to particulars as to *where* God reigns. He reigns over this world and holds it in His hand. Neither does the Psalmist specify enemies. He groups them all alike in one picture, the turbulent sea. And over all enemies alike, the Lord on high is mighty.

These truths are given to us as a shield and a strength. It's one thing to affirm that the Lord is King. It's another to take up that great truth and use it as a shield and buckler in the actualities of life. And as we cross from Psalm 93 to Psalm 94, that is the bridge we are crossing. There is a stopping place, and we are invited to put on armour – the truth that 'the Lord is King'.

2. Psalm 94: The King experienced

Having sat beside God, we can now come and sit in the world and view it in its proper proportions.

First of all, Psalm 94 brings us into *the place of difficulty.* The people of God find themselves an opposed people. In verse 3 the people of God are faced by their enemies, opposed in speech, acts and iniquities. How typical of the way in which the people of God suffer in this world! They suffer the defamation of the tongue, the persecution of the deed, and the opposition of unbelief. Verse 3 shows a particularly cutting form of disbelief. 'They say, The Lord shall not see, neither shall the God of Jacob consider.' It's not that disbelief which says God is not there. It's the disbelief that says God does not care. It's good that we have the situation set before us so that we can learn from the psalm the remedy and the recipe to apply.

And out of the place of difficulty the psalm brings us into *the place of prayer*. The psalm is a prayer. We might find the terms of it a bit abrasive – 'vengeance', twice in verse 1. Let me make it rougher for you before I make it easier: it's a plural noun, and so I believe it means total, dire, absolute vengeance. We might well step back from such a prayer because we don't like the idea of vengeance. They aren't terms that come easily in the mild and polite end of the twentieth century. It's therefore all too easy to say, 'Surely the Lord Jesus and the New Testament have taught us better. Mustn't we leave all that Old Testament stuff to one side?' Now I want to say to you firmly, that a dictionary can tell you what 'vengeance' and 'render to the proud their desert' mean, but only a concordance can tell you what the Bible means when it speaks of a God of vengeance. Bible words have Bible meanings. And I promise you, you don't need any Hebrew to grasp that. Now, with a concordance and patience, you will find that the meaning of the two words 'vengeance' and 'desert' appears to be: 'vengeance', 'that which is required in the situation'; and 'desert', 'that which is deserved'. All this is summed up in verse 2, in the appeal to God as Judge of the earth.

Note also, regarding the place of prayer, that this psalm is nothing *but* prayer. The psalmist does not intend to do anything about his enemies. He believes the Bible truth that 'vengeance belongeth unto the Lord.'

He proposes to do nothing about them in word, thought or deed except commit the case to God. And then note also that this is an effective way of dealing with the situation. Prayer is effective, and is given to the people of God as their first weapon when they face the antagonisms and hardships of life in this world.

Now thirdly, the psalm which brings us into the place of difficulty and the place of prayer brings us into *the place of reassurance*. Start at verse 8. 'Ye brutish' – that's the Revised Version – means man unchanged by the grace of God. It's got nothing to do with IQ. It has to do with those perceptions that only come through the Spirit. So we could say, 'Consider, you unregenerate ones . . . ' And the word 'fools' – it's a big word in Proverbs, and it means people who take a superficial view. The Psalmist appeals to them to see things as grace would enable them to see them. And in making that appeal he is spreading out before himself the situation as it is seen in the light of grace, to the discerning eye of the converted person. And this comes over as a message of reassurance to us. Verse 5 reassures us concerning *the God of redemption.* 'Thy people' – when and how did these people become the people of God? In Egypt. At the Passover. In the great work of redemption. And where in the Bible is this emphasis on care for the needy, the widow and the fatherless and the helpless? It's wrapped up in the Exodus theology, the Moses theology, the Book of Deuteronomy. The God of Exodus is the God who cares for the helpless. 'This,' He said, 'is My name for ever. This is how I am to be remembered for all generations. I am the Lord who brought you out of the land of Egypt.' Can He ever forget one on whose behalf the blood of the Lamb was shed?

And we have the reassurance of the *God of creation*. 'He that planteth the ear, shall He not hear?' God the creator (verse 9) is brought before us. The Old Testament sets out four ways that the Creator is involved in His creation: (a) He began all things; (b) He maintains all things; (c) He governs all things, and (d) He guides all things to their appointed destiny. Can that God be absent? Can he be uninvolved? The reassurance that comes out of the truth of God the Redeemer is, that His love will never fail us. His is a concerned involvement.

And thirdly as we are brought into the place of reassurance the psalm speaks to us of *the God of Providence* (verses 12 to 15). I use the word providence to remind us of God's direct involvement and direction and control, even to the smallest details of the experience of His people. What a marvellous verse is verse 12! A man opposed by hostile, God-denying enemies. They aren't afraid to speak out against God's people, to act against the helpless, to deny God's love. In the thick of that experience, he says 'Happy is the man whom Thou chastenest.' He speaks of that experience as a purposeful present, in which, verse 13 says, there are two components; it is the way to peace, the loving way that God brings His people home; and there is a pit being dug for the wicked. Verse 14 then tells us that in our present difficulties we can have an underlying confidence. 'The Lord will not cast off His people . . . ' And verse 15 takes the thought on into a future where righteousness will be established.

And then fourthly, the next element of reassurance is such a lovely one: *the God of tender care.* In verses 16 and 17, the Psalmist found himself afflicted by loneliness. 'Who will rise up for me . . . ?' There's nobody on his side. In verse 18, he found himself afflicted by the precariousness of life: 'When I said, "My foot slips".' And in verse 19 he found himself afflicted with distracting thoughts, pulled this way and that, not knowing what to believe – 'the multitude of my anxieties'. And in those situations, what did he find? He found *the Lord at his side.* Verse 17, I fear, can only be translated by an ungrammatical paraphrase; 'Except the Lord had been my help – Oh! what a help, and Oh, how definitely on my side.' Now no one in their senses would call that a translation! But that's how it feels.

And then, in verse 18, he found *the Lord at his need.* It's the other side of the story of the experience of the saint. On the one hand the certainty that the end has come; on the other the incessant mercy of God. And then he found that almost unspeakable thing, *the Lord in his soul.* 'In the multitude of my anxieties within me, thy comfort delights my soul.' Delight – it's only used about four times in Scripture. It's the word in the Hebrew which means: when you take a little one on your knee and cuddle him or her. The indescribable thing of the inner secret communications of God whereby He comforts His saint. It's the place of tender care.

And the last aspect of reassurance in this psalm is this: God is *the God of security and triumph.* I'm going to pass over the triumph – it's the triumph of God over the ungodly, He will cut them off – and I'm going to dwell on the security of the believer. Verse 22, 'The Lord has been my high tower and my God, the rock of my refuge.'

I'm going to dwell on that verse because I want to share with you two aspects of 'security' that come out of it. 'My high tower', and 'my refuge'. The first term speaks of security being made *unassailable. A high* place. The Lord lifts His child up into a sure refuge because it's high and inaccessible to the enemy. Therefore it's safe to flee to. The second term speaks of a security which is *available.* It is there to run to.

Safe to flee to: there to run to. The security that the believer has, in a God who is truly King.

2. Psalms 95 and 96: Tidings of salvation

Let's establish, first of all, a relationship between today's pair of psalms and yesterday's pair. In Psalm 93, we had 'The Lord is King': and in Psalm 94 we had the practical application, in giving God the title of Judge. Now Psalms 95 and 96 continue this entitling of our God: Psalm 95:3 'The Lord is a great God, and a great King,' and 96:10 (which almost amounts to the key phrase in this whole series of psalms), 'Say among the nations, the Lord reigneth.' (Which is an exact replica of 93:1). And in Psalm 96 the thought of God as Judge continues: 96:10, 'He shall judge the people with equity.' The verb, in whatever translation, is a verb meaning actually to settle disputes with people, to mend quarrels, to set people to rights. Then in verse 13 the same verb appears (as it did in 94:2), 'For He cometh to judge the earth.' When you realise, as you must do, that the expectation of a coming judge is in the context of a call to rejoicing (verse 11, 'Let the heavens be glad'), you'll realise that the verb 'to judge' doesn't carry with it the sole meaning of 'to pass sentence and condemn'. Here it has its basic Old Testament meaning of 'setting things to rights'. The Lord is going to come and set things to rights. So you see that here we have the same general area of teaching as in Psalms 93 and 94.

Now compare. In Psalm 93, the Lord's kingship was directly over the turbulence of this world – you will recall that very vivid picture in 93:3–4. Psalm 94 went on to express the effectiveness of the Lord's rule over His people, when they faced a stormy experience. Contrast 93:3 with the Lord reigning over the floods, and 95:3, 'For the Lord is a great God, and a great King above all Gods.' We are being led on in a progression. We have seen kingship over this world in the turbulence of history; now we are to see kingship over this world in the matter of the spiritual forces which are in this world and call forth allegiance. 'He is a great God, and a great King above all gods.' And 96:4 has the same emphasis on kingship. 'He is to be feared above all gods.' He is the King of gods!

Let's take up that thought as the first element in our study, taking Psalms 95 and 96 together for the moment. What does it mean when it says, *He is a King above all gods?* Notice that from 95:3 onwards and from 96:4 onwards the Psalmist isn't making a case out. It's an affirmation. It has, if you'll pardon this way of putting it, a 'Put that in your pipe and smoke it!' air about it. Insofar as 96:5 offers any explanation or justification for the statement of 96:4, it does so by making another statement. The Psalms go in for affirmation, not for arguments! And here they affirm the greatness of the Lord and His supremacy over any and every other spiritual power. Notice also that each psalm appeals to creation; so in 95:4, 'In His hands are the deep places of the earth; the heights of the mountains are His also. The sea is His, for He made it; and His hands formed the dry land.' One of the things you find in the Old Testament is that totality is often expressed by means of contrasts. See it here: 'deep places . . . heights of the mountains'; 'sea . . . dry land'. No matter how far you go up or down, it's all His, He made it. View the ocean, that's His, He made it; turn round and view the land, that's His, He made it. He is the Creator and He owns the lot. He's a great God.

In Psalm 96 the same truth is brought before us but this time in relation to the heavens, so the two psalms themselves together share this idiom of contrast in order that we might have a total view of God the Creator. Verse 5: 'For all the gods of the peoples are idols.' They're godlets. Hopeless, useless, ineffective. 'But the Lord,' continues verse 5, 'made the heavens.'

We ought for a moment to face the question: does the Bible believe that there is a multiplicity of gods? Many commentators on the Psalms really hold that it does. Well now, in fairness they ought to make the same accusation of Paul in 1 Corinthians 8:5 – 'Even as there are lords many and gods many'. Or against the dear writer of 1 John 5:21, 'My little children, keep yourselves from idols.' Do they believe there are many gods? You see they're all saying the same thing. They are saying that as a matter of religious fact there are powers abroad in the world that are claiming from people the allegiance due to the great God alone. The Psalmist looked at his world and he could see Baal and Molech and a howling crowd of others all claiming their devotees. It was essential for him to say in his context 'but the Lord is a great God and a great King.' He wished to draw his own people back from the enticement and entanglement of these other powers.

And, in contrast, the Bible makes the straightforward affirmation that there is one God and one Creator. How does the idea of one Creator point to the idea of one God? Well, the Psalms are poetry and are often allusive. We have to fill out some of these statements with what the rest of the Old Testament tells us, and therefore you must refer back to the four elements of creatorship that we identified at the close of our first study. And we see that He is a great, four-square God, originating, maintaining, controlling, directing.

Look for example at 95:4 to 5. 'In His hand are the deep

places of the earth.' Many people of that day would have said that the deep places belonged to the god Molech. No, says the Psalmist. It is the Lord who has the deep places of the earth in His hand. Similarly the heights of the mountains, and the sea, are made and owned by the Lord, not the destructive gods many held them to be governed by. Point by point the Psalmist challenges the reality of these other supposed gods. There is no Molech. There is no Baal – it is the Lord who reigns. People can be beguiled away, but they are beguiled by gods that are no gods. There is only one God, the great God and the great King.

Now, look with me particularly at Psalm 95. Let your eye run quickly down it.

1. Psalm 95: The only God, and His people

You see in verse 1, 'the rock of our salvation'. Note the pronoun 'our'. It is a psalm addressed to those who speak of God as 'our' Saviour. It belongs inside the church. Again, verse 6, 'Let us kneel before the Lord, our Maker.' Again, it's a psalm which belongs inside the people of God. And from verse 7 onwards it is a psalm addressed to those who have a history of the people of God behind them.

Now, see its shape – so often important in the psalms. Verses 1 and 2 are a call to worship. Verses 3 to 5 come as an explanation: why should we come and sing and worship so joyously? Answer: because the Lord is a great God. And in verse 6 the call is renewed. 'O come, let us worship and bow down.' We are called not to the joy of worship but to the reverence and self-humbling of worship, so well translated in the New International Version, 'Let us bow in worship.' They're verbs of 'coming down' – 'bowing in worship', 'bending the back', 'bending the knee'. Verse 7 is again an explanation (I do hope that your translation renders it as such, and verses

3 to 5 also). 'Today' – I like it in the Revised Version here – 'Oh that ye would hear His voice!' Why should we come so reverentially before Him? Verse 7 issues a different call – not to worship, but to obey. Verse 8 is an explanation and illustration in historical terms.

So that's the way the psalm is laid before us. A call to the *joyousness* of worship – then an explanation. A call to the *reverence* of worship – then the explanation. A call to the *reality* of worship – then the explanation.

This psalm may have been composed for the Feast of Tabernacles, a feast deeply related to worship and the kingship of God. In that feast the people of God were not only celebrating God's kingship. They were commemorating redemption, and the care God took of them in the wilderness, and they were warning themselves that they must open their hearts to the word of God. I want to look at these three elements of God as Saviour, Shepherd, and Lawgiver.

God as Saviour. The word 'salvation' that appears in verse 1 has a tremendous range of meaning in the Old Testament. But if the connection with the Feast of Tabernacles is right, then the salvation here is the saving act of God in Egypt. A *delivering* act – from slavery, into the state of free men able to walk before God; and secondly, a *spiritual* act, for He delivered them on Passover night from His own wrath and reconciled them to Himself. And thirdly it was a *supernatural* act, for on Passover night God said, 'On all the gods of Egypt I will take vengeance.' How suitable all that is to this psalm! The people speak of God as the 'Rock' of our salvation. What a magnificent and moving title that is. What does it speak of? Permanence. Reliability. Durability. He is a Saviour of that order. But I often think that there must be something more to it than that. The Psalmist is speaking of action – saving, overthrowing, bringing back – and 'rock' is a static image. Rocks don't, as a rule, *do* anything. Would it be possible, therefore, that already –

as he will be later on – the Psalmist is thinking of Exodus 17? What sort of rock is the Rock of Israel? 'Their rock,' said Moses in Deuteronomy, referring to the heathen gods, 'is not as our rock.' And in Exodus 17 the people murmured when they came to a waterless place, and Moses prayed. And God answered publicly, before witnesses. The rock was smitten and out of it came rivers of water for the deliverance of the people of God.

Now I can't prove what I'm going to say to you. Oh, the story was factual, that's great, I'm not trying to prove that. But I believe that ever after that, when the Old Testament speaks of God as the Rock, it means the stricken rock with the streaming side, from which – as if, to human eyes, by a miracle – there flowed that which was for the salvation and deliverance of the people of God. And, not I trust pressing the matter too fancifully, in Exodus 17, when God commanded Moses to strike the rock he said, 'I will stand before the rock.' So that when Moses struck the rock, he was striking it in the presence of God. Was the Lord so identifying Himself that in symbol it was out of the Lord Himself that salvation flowed? I can't prove it. But, my word! I like it.

God as Shepherd. We look forward from the place of kingship in verse 3 to the place of shepherding in verse 6. I think the word 'Maker' here refers to redemption rather than creation in the Genesis 1 sense. You'll find in a concordance that it's often used of the acts of God whereby He made this people His people. I think that's the meaning here. *He* is our God, and *we* are the people of His pasture. He is God our Shepherd.

There are three things here. *He is our God* – that's our security. Shepherds choose sheep. Sheep don't look after the shepherd. The shepherd looks after his sheep. God has taken us to be His people and committed Himself to our welfare. *We are the people of His pasture* – that speaks of a people who are provided for in His planning. A shepherd leads his flock from one pasture to another.

From one prepared pasture to another prepared pasture. *We are the sheep of His hand* – we are the individuals cared for in His love. By day the shepherd leads his flock. But when night comes he leads them to fold, and he stands by the door, and he examines each sheep as it enters and sees to its welfare.

God as Lawgiver. Verse 7 goes on out of that lovely pastoral scene to a very different one, a scene of command and call and requirement. Will you notice, please, the place that law has in the Bible? God saves a people, brings them into His care. Now, He says to them, this is how I want you to live. In the Bible law is not a ladder by which the unsaved try to climb into God's favour. It is a pattern of life by which the redeemed are required to live, in order that they may resemble and please the God who loved and redeemed them. The word 'law' in the Bible ought really to be translated 'teaching' – it's what happens in the loving context of a home. The God who saves and shepherds says this: 'Look, I love you enough to give you My law. I love you enough to tell you what I'm like so that you can live and be like Me. You are to be holy, because I the Lord your God am holy.'

'Harden not your hearts' – Oh, how serious law is in the purpose of God. You know the story of Massah and Meribah. In fact in this psalm there are three stories all crammed together. There's the one from Exodus 17, how the people grumbled and God paid no heed to their disbelief. There's the story from Numbers 14, how the spies wouldn't go back to the people because they disbelieved the promises of God. And in Numbers 20, where the people came again to a waterless place, and Moses struck the rock in disobedience and unbelief, and God said, 'You and Aaron must forfeit the right to lead the people into the promised land.' How seriously God takes His law. How seriously He views disobedience. Study those stories. And he calls on His people here to turn away from a hard heart, which, according to this psalm, is an unbelieving heart, an uninstructed heart. The common denominator to those three stories is unbelief. Why is this called 'testing God'?

I would suggest it this way. When they came to the waterless place, instead of believing God, they saw it as a test that they had to pass, in order to have it proved to them, that God is God. Verse 10 speaks of 'a people that do err in their heart, they have not known My ways.' Well, in one way they did know God's ways. They could have told you the whole story of how they came out of the land of Egypt. They knew it from A to Z, far better than we know it. They knew it in *one* way. But not in a *real* way. It wasn't changing their lives. Therefore their hearts were hard.

Now, briefly,

2. Psalm 96: The only God, and His gospel

Verse 2: 'Preach the gospel of His salvation from day to day.' Now I know it doesn't actually say that in your Bible; it doesn't say it in mine. I made it up! But that's what it means. This is a psalm about the gospel of God, the only God. It may be of advantage to you in your private study if we spend a moment looking at the shape of this psalm.

It starts off with a call to the world – 'O sing unto the Lord a new song: sing unto the Lord, all the earth.' A call to the world to worship. It goes on in the second half of verse 2 with a command to the church to tell; 'Preach the good news of His salvation . . . ' It continues in verse 4 with an explanation. Have you got that blessed word, 'because'? There is only one God.

Then, verse 7, a call to worship (the pattern's going to be repeated!) Verse 10, a command to the church to tell: and what they are to tell this time is a message of sovereignty and security. 'The Lord is King. The world is all right.' Sovereignty and security. And the reason why they are to go out with urgency with this message to the world is the explanation which is offered from verse 11 onwards. This great God, this only God, is coming to set the world to rights. So get right with Him before He comes.

So there's the pattern for you. Psalm 95: we are rejoicing in salvation. Psalm 96: those who rejoice in salvation must go and share it. Proclaim the good tidings of His salvation.

There are four elements of this proclamation: (a) it's *good news*; in verse 2 the world is called to 'bless His name'. (b) It's good news of *salvation*. 'Preach the message of His salvation from day to day.' Verse 3, 'Declare His glory among the nations, His marvellous works that He has done.' What is His message of salvation? It's a message of something God has done and in His glory declared. (c) It's good news of *reconciliation*. Verse 8 is a message which invites all the earth to come by means of the appropriate offering, right into the presence of God. That's good news. And (d) it's good news of *expectation* (verses 11 to 13). There is a forward look; back to the saving acts, forward to the coming God. Oh! to be there, the day that all creation comes to life, and the curse is removed, and the whole creation of God moves out into the liberty of the children of God. The day the trees begin to sing, because He comes. He comes to set everything to rights! Oh, may He come quickly. It's a gospel of expectation, for such a needy world.

I want to tell you that the outstanding impression from these two psalms – the only God and the gods: marvellous! – the only God and His people, great and challenging! – the only God and His gospel, heartwarming! – is the joy of the only God. The joy of those who know Him. Joy in a known Saviour. Joy in a God who has made Himself known as He is by telling us His name and His nature. The joy of knowing the only true God.

May that joy be our strength this day.

3. Psalms 97 and 98: Visible righteousness

These psalms obviously continue the themes with which we have become familiar. Psalm 97 begins with that key phrase, 'The Lord reigns.' And it has the same emphatic shape as the other occurrences of the phrase. The subject comes before the verb, which in Hebrew means that the subject receives a great shout of emphasis – 'It is the Lord who is King.' And there it is in 97:1. Notice a different expression of the same thing, in 97:5. The word 'Lord' means different things in this verse. The first time it appears in the verse it represents the divine name, the personal name of the God of the Bible, which in Hebrew is *Yahweh* and at some points in our English Bible appears as 'Jehovah'. The personal name – what I like to call God's 'Christian name'. The second time it simply means sovereign, or master. So this psalm continues the theme of the kingship of God. He is the sovereign of the whole earth, says 97:5. In 97:9 we read 'Thou, Lord, art most high above all the earth.' This is the title of Melchizedek's God, for he was a priest of God most high. I hope you remember what comes after that passage in Genesis 14: the definition of God most high as 'possessor, or creator, of heaven and earth'. This psalm is full of the idea of kingship and sovereignty. 98:6, a great shout to the great King.

And the idea of God as Judge also reappears here, in 97:2, the exercise of being a judge. And in 97:8, 'Zion heard and was glad, the daughters of Judah rejoice because of Thy judgement.' That is to say, 'Because you have exercised Your power and authority as King.' If I were to summarise the aspect of His kingship which comes before us in these two psalms, it would be: His kingship in the hearts and affections of His people. We shall be approaching that in the course of our study. For the moment, note simply that in these psalms the Lord's kingship is liked directly to a response of joy. 'The Lord is King. Let the earth rejoice' (97:1). This immediate response of joy is the new feature of these two psalms. Read 97:1, and then 98:8–9. Where kingship in, for example, Psalm 95, was linked only indirectly with joy, in these psalms the proclamation of the Lord as King excites an immediate, joyful response from the people who know Him to be their King.

It's all the more remarkable because these psalms have a strong emphasis on the darker side of the judgements of God, as we'll see. But you will notice also that the Lord's righteousness and His judgement and His holiness are brought to the fore – in their most threatening aspects in the opening verses of Psalm 97. Read verse 2, for example. We should note therefore that there is something remarkable in these psalms: that they couple together what for simplicity we can call the 'darker side' of the activity of the Lord as Judge, and the more threatening aspects of the righteousness and holiness of God; and at the same time they link the divine kingship with an immediate and exuberant response of joy from the people of God.

Part of the explanation – if we may continue a little longer in general comment on our two psalms – is that in these psalms we are invited to consider the completion of the work of God for His world. Compare Psalm 96 with Psalm 98. They are strikingly alike. Why, you might wonder, have two psalms so close together, that seem to say much the same thing? But look at the details and see how they balance each other. Psalm 96 belongs to our own time (verse 2, 'from day to day'), with the church going out to the whole world to proclaim the good news of salvation. But compare that with 98:2, 'The Lord has made known His salvation.' Gospel preaching has had its effect. Salvation is known (verse 3). Psalm 98 brings us to the end of the process when the work is done and the preaching accomplished, and the world knows the salvation of God. Psalm 96:3, His glory is to be declared; and verse 7, it is to be ascribed to the Lord. The nations are invited to respond in praise. In 97:6 we have a completion of that process: the heavens have declared His righteousness, and all the peoples have seen His glory. In our minds we are brought forward to the end. As we saw in the last study, part of the preaching is the preaching of expectation, of the coming Lord.

But when we come to Psalm 98:7, the world *has* responded and roars out its greeting to the King who is coming back. I notice that there is no response from the world in Psalm 96. There is response from the created order, but at that point there is no response from the world of men. And that is what 98:7 means. But the preaching of the gospel has produced a people waiting for the Lord, so there is a world of men ready to roar their acclamation to the King when he comes.

The balance of these two psalms is a mixture of joy and judgement and holiness which exactly matches the same mixture which is evident in the New Testament when it speaks of the return of our Lord Jesus Christ, and which will be the happy experience of those who are on earth when the Son of Man appears in the sky.

Let us now take up our course through these psalms and start in Psalm 97, where the first seven verses pick up the note of joy in its most surprising setting.

1. A joy co-existing with the grim reality of world condemnation

Just take into your mind verses 1 and 2. Notice, the Bible offers no connecting link. Verse 1, an earth rejoicing because God is King. Verse 2, 'Clouds and darkness are round about Him: righteousness and judgement are the foundation of His throne.' What is there in that to rejoice about? In order to see the contrast more starkly, compare verse 1 with verse 5 – a rejoicing earth; and verse 4 – a trembling earth.

Joy co-existing with condemnation. But it's a real joy, needing two different words to express it, meaning 'to exult' and 'to be happy'. Exultation and happiness. A true joy. Yet, alongside it, an earth that views the Lord and melts in His presence. Verse 2 gives us the picture of God's throne, drawn from Exodus 19, when God came to His people at Mount Sinai. He came wrapped in darkness and smoke, and though His coming among His people was a grace that they might meet with Him and hear his word, His coming was also the coming of the Holy One who said, 'Set bounds around the mount.' These clouds and darkness are expressive of a moral reality; 'righteousness and judgement are the foundation of His throne.' When the words 'righteousness' and 'judgement' come together in the Old Testament, they are balanced as follows: righteousness expresses principles, and judgement expresses practices. They are both manifestations of the holiness of God. The ideas come together in Isaiah 5:16, for example, where the righteousness of God expresses the principles of His holiness, and the judgement of God brings those principles down into application and action. God's throne rests upon the moral reality of principles of righteousness and practices of justice which expresses the holiness of the God who sits upon the throne. And, to the world, that is a picture of clouds and darkness, the threatening, judgemental side of the holiness of God.

Verses 3 to 5 speak of the light of God, but it is the light of God in the sense of His destroying presence. A fire goes before Him. Again, the Bible starts with the symbol, and fire is the symbol of the holiness of God, especially in its antagonism to sin. Fire excludes the sinner from the presence of the Holy One. When Mount Sinai was wreathed in smoke because the Lord had descended upon it in fire, the word was 'Draw not nigh hither.' Fire. The reality of a God in His spontaneous hostility to the presence of sin. In Isaiah 6, you will remember, as soon as the cry went up, 'Holy, holy, holy, is the Lord,' there was a spontaneous reaction in the rejection of the sinner Isaiah. The ground heaved, and smoke came down and blotted out the vision of God. Sin cannot dwell with holiness.

Verse 3: holiness is God's instinctive hostility to sin. Verse 4: His lightnings illumine the world – holiness in its universal manifestation. Verse 5: mountains melted like wax. Why? What did the Lord do? Beloved, He didn't do anything. He just came. The mere presence of God, and the whole physical world fabric begins to disintegrate.

So we have in the opening of Psalm 97 the righteous throne, the darkness of God, the destroying presence, the brightness of God. And in verses 6 and 7, the completed programme. The sense of the Hebrew text is of a completed act. 'The heavens have declared His righteousness. All the peoples have seen His glory.' The preaching of the gospel of God has reached its God-appointed terminus.

I think the reference to the heavens there means that the gospel has been officially and universally preached. The word has gone round the whole world. And God speaks of a universal opportunity that has been given; and, in verse 7, He points to a merited judgement. Look in your concordance for the verb 'ashamed' or the noun 'shame' in the Old Testament. I tell you, it means a great deal more than a passing sense of embarrassment. It nearly always has the meaning of reaping shame and disgrace. All those who have refused Him their loyalty, and have wedded themselves in loyalty to other gods, will reap the shame which is their portion. And the gods themselves, those seducers of the hearts and minds of men, will be cast down before the one who is a great King above all gods; and they will fall down before Him on that day as surely as the god Dagon fell before His ark in the land of the Philistines.

Now, my beloved, it is no joy to tell you these things, and it cannot be joy to hear them. But I leave it to you to judge whether I found these things in Scripture or whether I made them up myself. There it is; a joy, astonishingly co-existing with the grim reality of a world under divine judgement.

2. A joy facing the demands of holiness

In verse 8 and onwards to verse 12 we come to the second aspect of joy. Notice the theme again announced; 'Zion was glad, and the daughters of Judah rejoiced because of Thy judgement.'

Let us look briefly at the shape of the psalm. The psalm breaks itself up into two sections, by using the same two verbs – 'rejoice' and 'be glad' – to divide itself. Verse 1 matches 8 in a summons to joy. In verse 1 it's to the whole world; in verse 8, it's to the Zion people. They match right to the end. For example, verse 2 and verse 9, exaltation. Verse 3, speaking of adversaries, is balanced by verse 10, which speaks of lovers; verse 3 speaks of burning up, verse 10 of preservation. Verse 6 speaks of the manifestation of His glory world-wide; verse 11, of a glorious light laid up for the righteous. Finally, verse 7 speaks of those who reap shame, and verse 12, of those who enter into gladness in the presence of the Lord. I hope you find it satisfying to analyse your Bible and see it working like that! How deeply satisfying the word of God is.

But if you study that balance you reach this conclusion: that the world-wide people rejoicing in verse 1 must be the same as the Zion people rejoicing in verse 8! So we have here a reference to the eternal Zion, the mother of the people of God, the Zion in which every believer – according to Psalm 87 – has his citizenship. And it's a rejoicing people. Zion rejoicing in judgement. What a mystery! An undimmed joy, looking at the judgement of God. I do not understand it. It's one of the things that the Bible does not explain. At the end there will be those who fall under judgement and are lost. And yet, somehow, the joy of the people of God will be undimmed.

Yet a word of explanation is attached: 'because Thou Lord art most high over all the earth.' The people of God will be caught up in the vision of the glory of the supremacy of their God, who is most high over all the earth, and exalted far above all gods.

> Oh, the joy to see Thee reigning,
> Thee my own beloved Lord;
> Every tongue Thy name confessing,
> Worship, honour, glory, blessing,
> Brought to Thee with one accord.
> Thee, my master and my friend,
> Vindicated and enthroned,
> Unto earth's remotest end
> Glorified, adored, and owned.

It doesn't take away the mystery, but it goes far to explaining the joy.

Verses 10 to 12 describe the Zion people, in the form of an exhortation to them. 'O ye that love the Lord.' In the light of the coming end, the Psalmist can't but urge his people, 'If it's going to be like that, do make sure you're ready for it.' In the three verses 10, 11, 12, there are four factors. The first and last are things to do, the second and third are affirmations. That's the shape of the last bit of the psalm.

Let's look at the things to do, first. Firstly, there's a word for our emotions. 'Ye that love the Lord – *hate evil.*' This is what the Hebrew text says. It's a word to our emotions, a commitment, emotional and moral. The day that is coming is going to show in black-and-white the absolutes of God. As Paul says in Ephesians 5:5, 'No fornicator or unclean person or sexually lustful covetous man who is an idolator, has any inheritance in the kingdom of God and of Christ.' Christian ethics are eschatological ethics. That is, they derive their strength from what God will do on the last day in Christ. And at the last day, these will be the moral factors which will exclude; and God has set the seal of His absolute authority upon them. See, for example, 1 Corinthians 6:9. Eschatological ethics, for those who love the Lord.

And verse 12, '*Be glad*, ye righteous, *and give thanks to his holy name.*' Literally, give thanks to that which reminds you of His holiness. The mental activity of remembering. In remembering the name of God we are called to remember the meaning of that name (see Exodus 3:15). It is an indication of the sort of God He is. We are to remember, in the realities and difficulties of this life, that He is God the deliverer and redeemer; and we are to commit ourselves to Him, mentally and doctrinally, remembering His name, reminding ourselves of it, and acknowledging its meaning.

Then there are two things to believe. Firstly we are to *believe in His faithful deeds*. 'He preserves the souls of His saints; He delivers them out of the hand of the wicked. As the saints of God wait for the coming they commit themselves to Him, and He in turn commits Himself to them in a preserving grace which guarantees their continuance and rescues them from every adversary.

And verse 11, *'Believing His faithful promises'*. I will tell you the literal translation: 'Light is sown for the righteous, and gladness for the upright in heart.' I think the translators took fright, because they've never sown light in their gardens. But sowing looks forward to the reaping of a crop. God is not afraid of mixing His metaphors! Light stands for all that is joyous, all that relieves, all that uplifts, all that takes away and imparts happiness. God has *planted* it. And the day will come when His righteous ones will reap the crop. In the waiting days, as they wait for His coming, they rest upon the promise that the kingdom is there, that the joy is secure, and the consummation certain. The crop is on its way, and the harvest will come in the presence of the Lamb of God.

Psalm 98 verse 1 renews the call to joy. 'Sing unto the Lord a new song.' Once again, the theme is announced. Let's look first at the shape of the psalm. It rests on three exhortations. Verse 1, *'O sing unto the Lord.'* Verse 4, *'Make a joyful noise'* (or: shout aloud) *'unto the Lord.'* Verse 7, *'Let the sea roar.'* Three great invitations to make an enormous noise. Verses 1 to 3 are dominated by the word 'salvation'. In the Revised Version, the Revised Standard Version, the New English Bible and the Good News Bible, the word is translated 'victory'. But I'm going to stick to the word 'salvation', because the word looks back to the Rock of our Salvation in 95:1.

He has *wrought* salvation (verse 1); He has *made known* salvation (verse 2); All the ends of the earth have seen the salvation (verse 3). Well, when we're called to sing unto the Lord, there's no question what sort of God He is.

In verses 4 to 6, the second exhortation, 'Make a joyful noise . . . ' Again there's no question what these verses are about. Verse 6: the praising, hailing of the royal God.

And verse 7 introduces the third call to shout, and it is a shout in verse 9 – 'before the Lord, for He comes.' The praise of the saving Lord; the praise of the reigning Lord;

the praise of the coming Lord. A great paean of praise. The joy that comes from the Lord's kingship.

Now we'll look at the first three verses, and they bring us to the third aspect of the joy of the people who know their King. It is,

3. A joy resting upon a divine and finished work of salvation

Verse 1, *salvation accomplished:* 'He has wrought salvation.' It is supernatural; 'He has done marvellous things.' Again, only a concordance can help you. A better, more accurate translation would be 'supernatural things'. It's a salvation that only He could have wrought, as is emphasised in the next part of the verse; '*His* right hand, *His* holy arm, have wrought salvation for *Him*.' Not for us, for Him. What does that mean? Well, it means that salvation begins in the mind of God. The salvation of sinners is something God wants. Therefore it is done for Him. And also it is done in a way that matches His holiness. It sacrifices the character of God. And thirdly, 'His right hand' – it is done by His personal agency. Salvation accomplished by God.

Verse 2, *salvation revealed.* It is the divine intention to save. When God addresses men he addresses them in terms of their salvation. He doesn't wait for them to diagnose their need. He diagnoses and meets them with His remedy. And also, and just as in verse 1, his salvation meets the requirements of His own character. And thirdly, it is universal. It has been 'openly shewed in the sight of the nations'.

And, verse 3, *salvation experienced.* Where does salvation originate? In the mind of God. 'He remembered.' It originates in God's unprovoked love, the love we could never have imagined or provoked or deserved. It welled up in God's heart because He is like that. It has as its immediate purpose a chosen people: 'toward the house of Israel'. But it has as its ultimate objective the whole world: 'All the ends of the earth have seen the salvation of our God.' Salvation experienced. A joy that rests upon a divine and finished work of salvation.

And so our two psalms come to their end. I would translate verse 4 of Psalm 98, 'explode into song'. Why? Because, as the last four or five verses show, it is a joy consummated by the coming of the Lord. Every means is used: harps, singing, trumpets, cornets – every means.

Oh, at last! It's not just the voice of the sea and the inanimate creation given tongue, but there is a redeemed humanity. There is a church, there is the fruit of the gospel. There is a people to roar out their appreciation to a coming Lord, by every means, from every creature; to one focal point, 'before the King, the Lord'.

Because He comes.

4. Psalms 99 and 100: The Lord, holy and good

In our studies so far we have seen the kingship of God over the world – His actual kingship and His actual care of His people; then His kingship over the gods and spiritual powers which afflict and seduce the minds and hearts of men; and thirdly His kingship in the hearts and affections of His people. And right at the centre of that study, the call 'O ye that love the Lord, hate evil.' And now the spotlight falls in the only other place it can fall; on the kingship of God revealed in His own holy nature. We are shown in these two psalms why it is that God is King. The answer that is given is: He is a holy God,

Let's first of all show that the psalms do fit into the total statement of psalms 93 to 100. Psalm 99 starts with the key-cry, 'The Lord reigns', the subject coming first for emphasis. The second part of the verse tells us He is the enthroned God. In verse 4, there is again a reference to the King. Whatever translation we may have in front of us, we see that the two concepts of the King and the Judge are present. In verse 8, right at the end of the verse, we see the word 'vengeance', which we have dealt with before.

And all the truth of kingship which is so plain in Psalm 99 comes down three times over to the point of the divine holiness. It's an easy psalm to divide because it proclaims its own divisions. Like many hymns, it has a chorus; and though that chorus is a progressing, developing chorus, it has an identity. So: in verse 3, 'Let them praise Thy great and holy name. Holy is He.' In verse 5, 'Exalt ye the Lord our God. Bow in worship at His footstool. Holy is He.' And, in verse 9, 'Exalt ye the Lord our God. Bow in worship at His holy hill. For the Lord our God is holy.' It's a psalm of holiness, but the spotlight falls not on the King in His kingship, but upon the King in His holiness.

Now what about Psalm 100? Is it right to include it in the book of praises to the King? It doesn't make any reference to kingship at all. Why not stop at Psalm 99? Well first of all, because Psalm 100 brings Psalm 99 to its climax. It brings those three calls to praise God in Psalm 99 to their fruition in the two great invitations to come into the presence of God, 100: 1–2 and 4. And like Psalm 99 the spotlight is not upon the worshippers but upon the God they come to worship. The mind runs on in sequence from Psalm 99 to Psalm 100. But there's another reason Psalm 100 belongs with the book of the praises of the King, and that is, its plain link with Psalm 95. The expression 'We are His people and the sheep of His pasture,' which in Psalm 95:7 was a statement for the closed circle of the people of God, the Exodus people, in Psalm 100 has broken out of its old confines. We have seen, between the two psalms, the spreading gospel. So it is now the glad experience of a world-wide people who acknowledge this God, know His salvation, and rest in His shepherding care. So Psalm 100 brings the series to a climax, but it lifts up our eyes to the day to which we and the Psalmist look forward.

Let's come now to Psalm 99. As I have said, it divides itself, at verses 3, 5 and 9. Each section has its own emphasis. There is no doubt that the emphasis in the first three verses is on the greatness of the King, but I believe we will only grasp what this section is saying about the greatness of the Holy One if we allow ourselves to entitle it,

1. The grace of the Holy One

First and obviously, He is great. The Lord reigns. He doesn't have to do anything – He just *is*. And the Psalmist recognises that automatically, in the presence of such greatness, the people tremble. The mere fact of Him being King makes the whole earth move in His presence. He is great and high; He is awesome. His name as such spells fear in the hearts of men.

I am reminded of Joshua 2:9, where Rahab says, 'We know that . . . your terror has fallen upon us . . . because we have heard how the Lord dried up the water of the Red Sea before you when you came out of Egypt . . . and as soon as we heard it, our hearts did melt . . . because the Lord your God, He is God in heaven above, and on the earth beneath.' The awe-inspiring presence of God makes the hearts of men melt. 1 Samuel 4:7, another testimony from a foreign land: 'And the Philistines were afraid, for they said, "God is come into the camp." And they said, "Woe unto us, for there has not been such a thing heretofore. Woe unto us; who shall deliver us out of the hand of these mighty Gods?" '

Verse two adds, that He is near. It is a greatness at hand. He has brought down that awe-inspiring greatness into the indwelling position among His people in Zion. I'm reminded so much of Isaiah 6. Isaiah had a vision of the King in His holiness and he felt the earth tremble. And He suddenly knew in his own spirit the reality of the awe-inspiring nearness of the holy God.

But now look at that which occupies the centre of this section. He is gracious. Where does He set His throne, when he comes down to dwell? He sits enthroned upon the cherubim. Is this the enthronement that Ezekiel saw

(Ezekiel 10:20)? No, it is not. He *is* that, but not here. Is He enthroned above the cherubim of Genesis 3:24, that turned every way to guard the Tree of Life? No, no! This is the cherubim *in Zion*. So, what's that? We turn to Exodus 25:18. 'You are to make two cherubim of gold . . . and toward the mercy seat shall the faces of the cherubim be.' *That's* where he reigns enthroned. In the place of mercy. The grace of this great and awesome and near God, that when He comes down in all His greatness to be among His people, He takes up His throne in the place where mercy triumphs over wrath.

In verses 4 and 5 we turn to yet another theme.

2. The law of the Holy One

The literal translation of verse 4 is, 'The King's strength loves justice, or judgement.' Notice that all the strength of this great kingly God is wrapped up in the love and exercise of justice. The power of God has been wedded, in all love, to justice. 'The whole divine nature loves justice,' affirm these verses. And this links up with the fact that in the Old Testament, law is a manifestation of the image of God. Look at Deuteronomy 4:12; the image of God which the people were to treasure was the word that He spoke. 'You saw no form.' The Lord chose that He should be known among His people not by visible representation but by the law that He spoke to them. Go back also to Leviticus 19, where that amazing collection of laws is shot through with the refrain, 'I am the Lord.' It is the divine name. 'I am what I am.' If the people had asked, 'Why should we keep these laws?' the answer would come, 'Because the law represents among you what I am.' Therefore 19:12, 'You are to be holy, because I the Lord your God am holy.' The law is the perceptual image of God, and if anyone follows it he will be like God.

All the great strength of God goes out among His

people in concern for a just society. 'Thou dost establish equity.' Fairness between people. The implementing of holy principles and holy practices, judgement and righteousness. Both of these are the outflow of divine holiness. These are the concerns of God; a people who keep His law. And will you notice please that He insists on this, despite our incapacity. I was struck by the fact that it's Jacob who is mentioned here. As in 94:7, the name of Jacob is used, I believe, to underline the helplessness of the people of God, their inadequacy in their Jacob nature. It is of them that God demands life along the straight-edge of His law. He does not accommodate his principles to his inadequacies of His people. Rather, He says, obey the law, and it will minister life to you.

Did you know that, that the law, in God's hand is a means of grace? Read Leviticus 18:5. Its fulfilment had to wait for the full work of redemption of Christ. The counterpart of the Leviticus verse is Acts 5:13, which speaks of 'The Holy Spirit whom God has given to those who obey Him.' Obedience brings us into an experience of the power of the Holy Spirit.

But will you notice, before we leave these verses; the law of God is linked with the grace of God. He looks in Jacob for a standard of obedience which is beyond Jacob. He demands obedience from a people that constantly falls short. Read on, then. 'Exalt ye the Lord our God; and worship at His footstool.' If God is enthroned between the cherubim, where do His feet rest? How marvellous, that the verses which call us to an obedience which is beyond our capacity point us to a God who deliberately places His feet upon the mercy seat, where the blood is sprinkled. No sooner is the law declared than sacrifices are initiated, so that the blood of the lamb might accompany the people of God on their pilgrimage.

Truly the Bible is one book! 'If any man sin, we have an advocate with the Father, Jesus Christ the righteous.

And He is the propitiation for our sins.' Praise be to God, grace accompanies law.

Come now to the third section and again we're following in the line of holy kingship. This time we come down to the level of individual life; Moses, Aaron, Samuel (verse 6). They are representatives. We can look on them as typical of what it is like to be a member of the people of God. The theme of this section therefore is fellowship.

3. The fellowship of the Holy One

'Moses and Aaron among His priests' – what is the priestly privilege? Access. Going to God. 'Samuel among them that call upon His name' – what is the first characteristic of the people of God? They are a praying people, found in God's presence. And He answers prayer. The first mark of walking in fellowship with the Holy One is *a life of praying and receiving.* You will find that over and over again the hallmark of the people of God is that they are a praying people. Look in Psalm 138 where the Psalmist takes this truth even into the presence of other gods – 'Before the gods will I sing praises unto Thee.' It has the feeling – do pardon me – of 'I'm going to spit in your eye, because *you* can't do these things.' The God of Israel is a God who hears and answers prayer.

A life of praying and receiving; and then, verse 7, *a life of hearing and obeying.* The people of God come out of the secret place and begin to turn their faces toward the public place. Look at the interchange in verse 7 between 'They' and 'He'. Do you see the fellowship of it?

The second mark of those who walk in fellowship with their God is the hearing and obeying of an accredited and a normative revelation. An accredited revelation, because so insistent was He that His people should have an accredited revelation that God came down as the Word, and set His hallmark on the written word of God. A normative revelation, because behind the idea of 'statutes' is the idea of permanence. The word of God is authenticated by Himself, and is graven in the rock to become for the people of God the permanent norm and standard of the way they think and act.

And the third mark of those who walk in fellowship is *a life of forgiveness and chastisement.* Let's open up that idea of forgiveness first. Literally: a God of sin-bearing. From Psalm 99 look back to Leviticus 16:22, when on the Day of Atonement Aaron the priest takes the live goat – the sin-bearer. Look forward to Isaiah 53:12, 'He poured out his soul unto death, and was numbered with the transgressors, and bare the sin of many' – same word. 'The Lamb of God,' says John, 'who bears away the sin of the world.' The Bible is one book.

'Thou wast a God' – sin-bearing; yes, but You were also a God taking vengeance. Giving exact payment for wrong done. So it was when Moses and Aaron disobeyed God in the smiting of the rock. They were excluded from the land. Not one or the other but both, forgiveness and vengeance. Forgiveness without vengeance would make us complacent; chastisement without forgiveness would crush us. Together, they are the guarantee that while we can trust we will be forgiven, we can never take sin lightly. A God of forgiveness and chastisement. The fellowship of the Holy One.

And so to Psalm 100. Here is the sum of all privilege; to be with Him, to know Him.

4. The people of God in the presence of God

Let's as usual take a look at the shape of the psalm. It's all sewn together beautifully. It starts with a threefold invitation. Verses 1 and 2, just pick out with me the three verbs. Three commands, or invitations. Verse 1, 'Make a joyful noise.' Verse 2, 'Serve with gladness.' The end of verse 2, 'Come before His presence.' The threefold invitation is followed by a threefold affirmation: (a) 'Know that the Lord is God,' (b) 'It is He that made us, not we ourselves' (c) 'We are the people, the sheep of His pasture.' It focuses attention upon the works of God.

Then verse 4, a threefold invitation. Pick out the verbs again. 'Enter His gates with thanksgiving, His courts with praise.' 'Give thanks to Him.' 'Bless His name.' A threefold invitation, followed by a threefold affirmation. Because – verse 5:1, 'the Lord is good'; 'His mercy endures for ever,' and 'His faithfulness is to all generations.' Now isn't that beautiful?

Now take up the first invitation with its accompanying affirmations. It speaks to us of *the privilege of access.* The three verbs are of increasing access to God. 'Shout' – 'Serve' – 'Come into His presence.' We hail Him from afar, we worship Him, and then we come right to where He is. We come to stand before Him. The privilege of access; the people of God welcomed into the presence of God. And they come with joy. The joy of their approach is explained by three facts. How can they come rejoicing? Because of what He has done for them. Look at Him, the God of Israel, the God we know by name. What has He done for us? He made us. I'm going to treat that verb as I did with it in Psalm 95: I'm going to treat it as referring to the redeeming works of God. Not a reference to creation but redemption. Those who were formerly sinners and lost became the redeemed people of God. And if that were not cause enough for rejoicing, He is our shepherd, we are His people, the sheep of His pasture.

So we look forward and see Him as God; backward, and see the work of salvation He has wrought, and around, to see His shepherding care. And we rejoice that we belong to Him.

The second half of the psalm, verses 4 and 5, speak of *the privilege of intimacy*. Again, three verbs of increasing closeness. 'Enter His gates' – come through, into the nearer presence, look up and 'give thanks to Him.' But then, come closest of all, and 'bless His name.'

How can *we* bless God? Well, what does He do, when He blesses us? He examines our situation and reacts accordingly. He reviews what we are and responds to what He finds. How do we bless God? Why, we review what He is and respond to what we find. 'Therefore,' says the Psalmist, 'bless His name.' Ransack the revelation of Himself that He has given and encapsulated in His name. Explore from one end to the other, and let your mind and heart be drawn out in worship and adoration and commitment and in every other way, that the fathomless nature of the eternal God requires. Bless His name.

But what, in particular, do we find, as we ransack His name? The affirmation in verse 5 dwell on what God is, the nature of God. We find that the Lord is good; that His mercy is for ever, and His faithfulness is for all generations. We look at Him as He is, and we find that He is essentially, wholly, completely, utterly good. We look at Him in His unvarying attitude toward us, and we find that His steadfast love is everlasting. And we look at the ongoing experience of life, and we find that His faithfulness, His reliability, just goes on and on; one generation after another in the unvarying experience of the people of God.

I can't think of any better way to end such a psalm as that than the way familiar to many of us using the psalms in worship, bringing each psalm – but surely, surely these two specifically – by saying,

'Glory be to the Father, and to the Son, and to the Holy Ghost, as it was in the beginning, is now, and shall be for ever. World without end, Amen.'

THE CHRISTIAN WAY OF LIFE

by Rev. Eric Alexander

1. Romans 12:1–13

Romans 12 to 15 is that section of the Epistle that contains so much of Paul's ethical teaching, and we're going to study it in these four readings under the general title of 'The Christian way of life'. In a sense, another title could be what the founders of the Keswick Convention called 'scriptural, personal, practical holiness.' We greatly need to consider the ethical challenge of biblical holiness (which is always *practical* holiness), and apply it to our whole way of life. So what we shall be doing is seeking to discover the practical implications of that full salvation which God had provided for us in Jesus.

One or two introductory matters as background to our study. Firstly, context. If you wanted one word to summarise the theme of the Epistle, I think that word would have to be 'righteousness'. In four areas Paul expounds this: 1–3:20, *righteousness lacking in man* (3:10 is a key verse); 3:20–8:39, *righteousness provided by God* (5:17 is a key verse with its emphasis on the 'free gift'); 9:1–11:36, *righteousness rejected by Israel* (and here 10:3 is a key verse); and then 12:15–15:13 – which ends the main section of the Epistle – *righteousness manifested in the life of the redeemed.* (14:17 would be a key verse). So there's Romans in a nutshell!

The importance of that context is brought out by that little word at the beginning of 12:1, 'therefore'. Paul's ethical teaching does not start at chapter 12, where he begins to speak of Christian behaviour. It grows out of the whole exposition of the gospel in chapters 1 to 11. The New Testament knows nothing of a truncated ethical system outside of the gospel. It's been said that you cannot separate Paul's *ethical imperatives* – that is, the demands of the gospel – from his *doctrinal indicatives* – the statements of the gospel. For without the gospel of redeeming grace, the imperatives become just a counsel of despair. From the kind of religion that says 'All you need to do is live by the Sermon on the Mount and the Ten Commandments, and do as much of it as you can,' we recoil saying, 'What I need is not a lecture, but a Saviour.' The unique distinctive thing about the New Testament ethics, you see, is that the New Testament provides a dynamic for fulfilling them.

What then is the point of these ethical directives? It's simply this; if the ethic needs a dynamic for its fulfilling, the dynamic needs an ethic for its guidance. You need the work of God's sovereign grace to make you a new man in Christ – that's the steam in the boiler of a locomotive, if you like – and then you need the ethical directives to guide you into the Christian way of life – putting the locomotive on the right rails. 'Our consciences,' says Dr Packer, 'are not educated by gospel but by law.' It's part of the bigger question of the relationship between law and gospel in the whole of Scripture, never expressed better than by the Puritan Samuel Bolton: 'The law drives us to the gospel to learn how to be saved, and the gospel sends us back to the law to learn how to live.'

The other thing I want to say by way of interest is that Paul is in these chapters still speaking of salvation. For biblical salvation deals with a moral transformation in our character, not just a change in our destiny. Indeed the section to which we turn is really Paul's invitation to enter into all the implications of what God has done for us in Christ. It's not some advanced stage of spirituality attained to by the few; it's the beginning of Christian commitment, it's of the essence of true repentance and faith.

You will notice that verses 1 and 2 begin not with a discussion about the 'Christian attitude' to this or that, but with a summons to consecrate our bodies as a living sacrifice to God. The key to the Christian attitude in every issue is: clarity in consecration of ourselves wholly to God. You cannot understand the true Christian attitude to anything, outside of this. So we shall have to spend a considerable time on these first two verses, which are quite crucial.

1. Verses 1 and 2: a summons to consecration

Paul uses the strong word variously translated 'I appeal to you', 'I call upon you', 'I urge you', 'I admonish you', 'I call upon you and beseech you'. We need to look first at the *ground* of this appeal and then at the *nature* of it.

The ground of the appeal. The ground of this appeal to a consecrated self-offering to God is 'by the mercies of God'. It refers to the whole history of God's dealings with sinful men expounded already in Romans 1 to 11. It refers to the whole scope of what He has done for us in Jesus Christ, and chiefly in His atoning sacrifice and self-offering on the cross. Paul's point is that it's only when we have explored something of the depths of God's mercy shown in Jesus, that this summons to consecration will find an answer in our hearts that is acceptable to God. Let me put it like this: the reason for trivial, superficial Christian living in ourselves or others is almost always a trivial, superficial view of the sin-bearing death of Jesus. Have you not grasped, says Paul, what redemption means? He applies the truth in his epistles. Do you not know, he says, that you were bought with a price? . . . 'Men will never worship God,' said John Calvin, 'with a sincere heart, or be roused to fear and obey Him with sufficient zeal, until they properly understand how much they are indebted to His mercy.'

The ground of Paul's appeal is the infinite mercies of God, which have found us in such a state of desolation and judgement and have raised us into a state of such blessedness that we have this great testimony: we have been to the fountain that God has opened for sin. We have tasted that the Lord is gracious, we have been justified by His grace, redeemed from sin's bondage, saved from God's wrath, adopted into His family and assured of everlasting life. God has taken us out of the kingdom of darkness when we were enemies of Him, and adopted us – all out of His infinite mercy. It's important to see that the ground of salvation is not a thing that *I* have done but solely the mercy of God, in Jesus Christ. That's not merely a doctrinal issue! It's an issue for practical Christian living.

The nature of the appeal. There are two elements in this appeal. In verse 1, it is *the sacrificial offering of a body to God*. The language here is clearly the language of sacrificial ritual. In the Old Testament there were two kinds of sacrifice; there were *propitiatory* sacrifices to atone for sin, such as were offered on the Day of Atonement, and there were *dedicatory* offerings arising out of an experience of God's goodness. Think of it like this; Paul has dealt with the fulfilment of the propitiatory sacrifices in chapters 1 to 11; now, in the second half of Romans he turns to the implications of dedicatory sacrifices. And what he says about this sacrifice first of all, is that it's the offering of a body to God.

Now it's often said that 'body' here symbolises the totality of man; his personality, character and so on. And clearly Paul doesn't intend to restrict this consecration just to the physical body. But equally there's a suggestion here, in the way Paul uses the word, that it's mainly the physical body that Paul is speaking about. And this is important. The Greek philosophers depreciated the body – the ideal was to get rid of the body altogether. But the biblical view of salvation runs deeply counter to that. God created us in bodies bearing His image, and when He glorifies us at the end of the age it will be in new bodies that we will serve and worship Him. The Christian hope is in the resurrection of the body. So, sanctification must include the body.

Christ is our pattern here. When He consecrated Himself to our salvation He took His body and offered it to God. True Christian consecration is never a nebulous, mystical, impractical thing, and that's why New Testament teaching about the Christian way of life reaches down to practical details of what you do with your tongue, eyes, hands and so on.

Note also that it is to be a *living* sacrifice. The Old Testament offerings, because they were symbols of divine judgement, were slain. Our sacrifice is to be living, so that our bodies might become the vehicles of the divine will and our lives the object of the divine pleasure. Such offering is our 'reasonable service' (AV), but it seems to me that the Revised Standard and New International versions have caught Paul's intentions better with 'spiritual worship'. And the New American Standard Version puts the two together: 'your spiritual service of worship'. Now that's a good translation, because Paul is probably contrasting the outward ceremonial worship, offering an unwilling slain animal to God, with the inward spiritual worship of a willing, rational living being to Him. This of course is a great deal of help in understanding the real nature of worship, and Paul at the end of verse 1 does seem to be referring to the common worship of God's people. True worship, says Paul, (a) derives from a proper view of God's grace in Jesus Christ and is a response to it; (b) is intended to engage our minds;

(c) is the presentation of our bodies as a living sacrifice to Him; and (d) is spiritual, engaging the heart. Genuine spiritual worship.

And the second element of this consecration is *the gradual transformation of our character by God.* The appeal of verse 2 is based on the fact already expounded by Paul, that the new age, as it were, has dawned for the Christian. He is to be fashioned, not according to the passing fancies of this world, but according to the patterns of glory which belong to the world to come. The great temptation, you see, is to be conformed instead of transformed; it happens in all sorts of subtle ways, often subliminally. You can take up attitudes and standards and criteria, particularly, I would suggest, through the pressure of the media. Have you noticed how easily your spirit becomes inured to the frequent adultery you hear about? The apostle is saying: do not be conformed to this world, but be transformed by the renewing of your mind. Jesus warned, 'Do not be like those who seek the things of this world. Seek ye first the kindom of God, and His righteousness.' Be being transformed (that's the literal translation, implying what Lenski called 'a constant inner metamorphosis'). The Greek word translated 'transformed' is the word used for our Lord's transfiguration. Interestingly, the only other usage is in 2 Corinthians 3:18: 'We all with open face beholding as in a glass the glory of the Lord, are being changed' – metamorphosed, transfigured – 'from one degree of glory to another.'

Now this is what Christian character is all about. We are being changed into the image of His glory. And the transfiguration of Jesus is in some ways a pattern of that, and it is to transfiguration we are called.

Now the means of such a moral transformation. Verse 2: 'by the renewing of your mind'. The primacy of the mind in biblical sanctification is a great biblical principle. I wonder if you've noticed, that the old order finds sin making its appeal through the senses – the tree was good for food, pleasing to the eyes, and a tree to be desired. Whereas the new order in Christ makes its primary appeal through the mind. 'Be not mindless, but understanding what the will of the Lord is.'

Now that leads us to the last part of verse 2: 'that ye may prove what is the will of God'. There are two ideas in the word 'prove'. One is, 'discerning in our understanding'; and the other, 'discovering in our experience' – what the will of God is. How do we come to know the will of God, in these two senses? The basic means is the consecration of ourselves to Him. The specific means is the renewing of our minds.

First: a disposition to do the will of God is always the basic key to discovering it. We prove the will of God by presenting our bodies a living sacrifice to Him. And the second point is that we do not primarily discern the will of God by hearing voices or 'feeling led'. Scripture makes primary the relationship between the will of God and the mind of the believer so that we may think our way through to the mind of Christ. How much we need to be reminded of this today!

Some of us have a deep-seated suspicion about the will of God, deeply rooted in our character. We say, 'If it's the will of God, I must resign myself to it.' Beloved, in Scripture the will of God is something to be run after, to be pursued like gold, because it is so good and perfect and acceptable for His children!

2. Verses 3–13: in the church we are to be good brothers

Having laid the foundations in verses 1 and 2 (as I said, we have spent a great deal of time on them), Paul turns, in 12:3–13:17, to three spheres of living and testing. In outline, he says: in the church we are able to be good brothers; in the world we are to be good neighbours; and in the State we are to be good citizens. In the remainder of this study we will be looking at the first of these.

In the church we are to be good brothers. Immediately, at the start of verse 3, Paul establishes the apostolic authority by which he speaks. Do you notice that phrase, 'the grace given to me'? Quite clearly this is not grace in the general sense but the grace of apostleship, and the appeal of verse 3 has to be seen in the light of the appeal of verse 1. In verse 1 the appeal is on the basis of divine mercy, but in verse 3 it is on the basis of apostolic authority. These appeals are equally binding. That enshrines a very important principle; it means that Paul's words bear the authority of God. That's what the apostolic truth and authority implies; God has given to the apostles the special responsibility of formulating gospel truth, and the result is in – and constitutes the authority of – the New Testament. So you see we must acknowledge the authority of Paul. It is a vital principle for the authority of Scripture that authority is given to the apostles. And the doctrine of authority of Scripture rests partly on this apostolic authority.

Now Paul, having established this, goes on in verse 3 to point out that so often our thinking about ourselves is wrong. J. B. Phillips translates: 'Don't cherish exaggerated ideas of yourself, or of your own importance.' One of the evidences of God's grace working in a man's life will be seen in a new attitude to himself. This is where grace changes the whole direction of our thinking and living. 'He died for all,' says the apostle in 2 Corinthians 5:15, 'that those who live should no longer live to themselves but unto Him, who died for them and rose again.' I am increasingly persuaded that this brings us to the core of what the Christian life is all about – godly, biblical humility.

But, you notice in verse 3, the biblical alternative to an inflated view of ourselves is not a false depreciation of ourselves, but 'to think with sober judgement . . . ' Now that's important, because often people think that Uriah

Heep, in Charles Dickens' writing, is the closest example of biblical humility – 'I'm an 'umble man, Mr Copperfield,' he kept saying. Of course he didn't really believe it. There's often a way to puncture that kind of attitude – you just agree with it! People don't want you to agree with their 'Heepishness'. And it's not biblical.

To think with 'sober judgement' means that the renewal of our minds will produce a realistic assessment of ourselves. We will have the grace to come to terms with how God made us and His providence has shaped us, becoming neither pompous bores nor grovelling hypocrites. And the significant thing about verses 3–8 is that the place where this is best achieved is in the true God-given diversity of a living fellowship of God's people. That's why the two key words for finding yourself are 'grace' and 'faith'. The central statement of the passage is in verse 6, 'Having gifts that differ according to the grace given to us . . . ' Now that means that whatever good there is in us is the work of God's grace. How can *I* be inflated by this? It is the grace of God which has produced my gifts, and therefore I am able to recognise that. I can avoid the blasphemous affront of using God's gifts as a means of self-display. The true seedbed of biblical humility is the doctrine of grace.

Now, you will notice that in the gifted body of Christ there is equality of dignity and diversity of function, compared in verses 4 and 5 to the human body. Our own God-given function is discovered by a recognition of God's grace, and an exercise of God-given faith. Notice the end of verse 3 – 'according to the measure of faith . . . ', and verse 6, 'in proportion to our faith'. (Probably not so much saving faith, as serving faith.)

This means that I must beware not only of pride, but of unbelief. That's important for our own well-being, for it helps us to become truly ourselves. And it's important for the well-being of the church, for the church will never become what God meant it to be, if, through unbelief, I am settling for being less than what God meant me to be. It's the glory, you see, of that picture of the body. And you have a place in that body. You dare not, by unbelief, miss God's place in it for you.

So Paul urges every member of the body (verses 6–8) to exercise precisely the gift that God has given them. The list of gifts is not really a list of offices, but a series of examples to show how varied the gifts are and how they are to be exercised. Do you notice that there are seven in all? Two directed to the gift itself, and two to the person. '. . . If prophecy,' (verse 6), 'let him prophesy in proportion to faith; if service, in serving.' These are the gifts themselves. Then follow the persons – he who exhorts, contributes, gives aid, etc. The gifts are to be exercised again in proportion to faith. The correct translation is probably, 'According to the proportion or analogy of *the* faith'. And I think that Paul is quite simply saying here that whatever is uttered as coming from God must be consistent with the rest of revealed truth. To the prophet he says: don't go outside God's truth. Then, service; probably a reference to the deacons. Then teaching, the expounding of revealed truth. Let the teacher stick to his last, says Paul; be not a speculator but an expositor. The exhorter, suggests the New International Version, is possible the encourager. He who contributes – this is a reference to personal giving, not to the official church collection. Let it be without mixed motives, Paul is probably counselling. The sixth gift is 'giving aid' (RSV), but it's probably leadership. How much we need that gift to be exercised in the church today.

The last gift is the showing of mercy, which is really that quality of godly care which ought to mark a real fellowship. If that is *your* gift, says Paul, exercise it with cheerfulness. And how helpful it is, when people have found their way into God's perfect destiny for them in this sense.

Verse 9 marks a new section of the chapter. It is a

turning of our attention manwards, into the area of relationships, where our sanctification is so often tested. Verse 9 lays down the universal obligation, having spelt out the diverse gifts. 'Let love be genuine.' That love is of course a divine and not a human thing; a supernatural, rather than a natural grace; the first fruit of the Holy Spirit. It's the hallmark of discipleship, according to Jesus. 'By this shall all men know that you are My disciples, if you love one another.' The whole thought of verses 9 to 13 is really of a life which goes out to others in selfless devotion and service. Notice these things about this love. First (verse 9), it must be real, without hypocrisy. It must be moral. It must be zealous for the good of others. Secondly, (verses 10 and 11) it is a driving zeal to love and care. Paul brings this to a great climax at the end of verse 13, where he speaks of hospitality. What is this love in relation to others that is to be seen in our lives in consecrated Christian living? It is hospitality. That word belongs to the same family as 'hospital', the place for the care of sick and wounded. What Paul is pleading for is a life that is a hospital for the sick and wounded and needy in the world. That's what consecrated Christian living really means in relation to others.

God make our lives like hospitals!

2. Romans 12:14–13:14

1. Verses 14–21: in the world we are to be good neighbours

Now the apostle broadens his focus to include the wider world around us; the unbelieving and frequently hostile world. Verse 9, as we have seen, introduces love as the universal obligation that we owe both to our fellow Christians in a 'family' sense, and to the world even when it persecutes us. This is what is to control all our relationships. You will notice tremendous similarities and parallels with the Sermon on the Mount. 'Love your enemies,' says Jesus (Matthew 5:44): 'Bless those who persecute you,' says Paul (verse 14). Bless, in Scripture, means different things. When we bless God, we give Him the praise and glory which He deserves. When God blesses us, He bestows on us the grace which we do not deserve. When we bless other people, we desire for them the riches of God's grace irrespective of what they deserve. That's what it means to bless those who persecute you. The second half of the verse reinforces this with an appeal that the blessing should be whole-hearted and not half mixed with cursing. You remember James' warning, about the mouth out of which proceeds both blessing and cursing? What Paul is saying is that the attitude we are to have to our enemies who persecute us is unmixed desire for their blessing, ruling out bitterness and animosities and harboured resentments. This of course is precisely what Jesus teaches in the Sermon on the Mount, and the reason he gives is, 'that you may be children of your father'. In other words – this is what God is like. 'I grant,' says Calvin, 'that this is hard and quite contrary to human nature; but there is nothing so arduous that it cannot be overcome by the power of God. And this we shall never lack, provided we do not neglect to pray for it.'

The results of this basic attitude described in verse 14 are to be seen in our obedience to the demands of verses 15 to 21. For example, verse 15; if I desire God's blessing on somebody, then I will genuinely rejoice when they receive it, and genuinely mourn when they are denied it. That is something the world never does. It is supernatural to rejoice, with no tinge of jealousy, when others are being blessed, particularly if we do not like them. And it is a very important test as to whether we are concerned for the glory of God or for our own little ego or little show. We need to pray that God will give us that detachment from other things, for His glory.

This reinforces to us how utterly vital it is to transform our attitudes, because so much of the teaching up to the end of chapter 12 depends on a spirit of self-forgetfulness. And that spirit depends on three things of which verse 16 particularly speaks. Firstly, *disharmony.* 'Live in harmony with one another,' says verse 16; and Lenski points out that this is a harmony deriving from something deeper than unanimity of mind. I am to want for you what, if I were in your position, I would want for myself. Self-interest, you see, destroys harmony. Think what our fellowship would be like if we were really desiring for others what we would most like for ourselves, were we in their position! Then, *snobbery.* 'Do not be haughty, but associate with the lowly.' The tendency in a godless world is to aspire to the society of those you conceive to be above you and to despise those you conceive to be below you. It's self-interest, again. It's perilously easy to harbour that spirit secretly, even if we would never openly admit to it. I have no hesitation in saying that all forms of snobbery are obnoxious to the God who was born in a shed, raised as a manual worker, and for much of His life was homeless and of no fixed abode. You can't sanctify snobbery. You can only mortify it.

The third thing that self-forgetfulness rules out is *vanity.* I'm inclined to think that what is meant is intellectual vanity – snobbery applied to wisdom. Closely allied to it is conceit, which makes it impossible for us to learn from others.

You can see how each of these derives from self-interest. Moving out into every sphere of life, self-interest affects us in these various ways, and these are the three areas the apostle puts his finger on.

Now verses 17 to 21 take this attitude of self-forgetfulness and apply it to the case of the Christian who has suffered injury or abuse of some sort or other, and explain how he is to react to it.

Of course these verses have often been misunderstood and misapplied and misused as a biblical basis for rejecting retributory punishment, that is, punishment as the just reward for wrongdoing. People often quote, 'Repay no one evil for evil.' Also they are used to reject capital punishment. Now whatever you think about capital punishment, you can't deduce a view of it from these verses, that's what I want to say. I want to suggest to you that these verses are not concerned really with such issues at all. The misunderstanding arises from a failure to grasp that these verses speak of personal relationships, not the public administration of justice to which we come in chapter 13. It's a distinction that needs to be carefully kept in mind.

There are two great principles in these verses which Paul sets down for us, beginning in verse 17. Firstly, *the Christian must never behave as though he were a law court* exacting justice: 'Repay no one evil for evil' – that is, getting your own back. And, in its place, in the second half of verse 17, a spirit which is concerned for a standard of conduct which will commend Christ to our unbelieving neighbours. Instead, 'take thought for what is noble in the sight of all.' And of course the example is Jesus who, when He suffered, threatened not. The corrollary to the principle of not behaving as if one were a law court is that the law court itself must never behave as if it were an individual, dealing with personal relationships and not matters of public justice.

The second great principle that Paul raises is, *the Christian must never behave as though he were God,* taking vengeance (verse 19). Vengeance is a function that God has reserved exclusively for Himself. There are occasions when we find our patience tried. Is that not so? We cannot understand how people 'get off with this kind of thing,' as we say. Of course this is the age-old problem of the ungodly, with which the Psalmist wrestles in Psalm 73. The biblical command, you see, is to leave it to God. Now failure to do that is really the kind of unbelief which shows that we are not sure enough of God to be able to trust Him for this – that we are more sure of ourselves, and our ability to take matters into our own hands. Professor Murray sees this issue as touching the essence of piety, which, he says, is 'turning everything over to God.' Whereas the essence of impiety is to try to take the place of God and take things into our own hands.

Instead of acting the law court or acting God, therefore, we are to act the peacemaker (verse 18). It may not always be possible, but Paul says 'if it be possible'. 'The most peaceful Christian,' wrote Martin Luther, 'may be set upon by snarling, biting dogs.' Paul's point is, that if peace *is* broken, you should never be the cause of it for your own sake. 'Blessed are the peacemakers,' says Jesus, in terms of personal relationships. We need to ask ourselves: am I the kind of person in a fellowship who is a peacemaker, or a peacebreaker? The cause of disquiet and unrest is so often our wounded pride or our thoughtless selfishness.

Finally, says Paul, we are to act the conqueror (verses 20 and 21). Paul moves from the negative attitude, the refraining from acting against our enemy or maintaining the peace, to the positive act of seeking to change him. How? That's the great question. If we show the same attitude to the worldling as he shows to us, he has conquered us. That's all that has happened. You know, you go away, and then – 'Oh, if I'd just thought of that cutting barb I could really have pierced him with – but I thought of it too late, I always think of the right thing too late!' Why is it? Because you wanted to satisfy your selfish pride, that's why. But if you had remembered, he would have conquered you, not you him. So Paul says, 'If your enemy is hungry, feed him; if he is thirsty, give him to drink, for by doing so you will heap coals of fire on his head. Do not be overcome by evil, but overcome evil with good.' That's the significance of the phrase 'heap burning coals upon his head' (a phrase which is a quotation from Proverbs 25, verses 21 and 22).

2. Chapter 13 verses 1 to 7: in the State we are to be good citizens

This is a new direction which the apostle takes in considering the Christian way of life, and chapter 13 can be seen as containing three obligations linked to three themes. 1–7, *the theme of authority and our relationship to the State;* 8–10, *the theme of love and our obligation to the law to fulfil it;* and 11–14, *the theme of the return of our Lord and our obligation to holiness in the light of it.*

We turn now to the theme of authority and the obligation of civil obedience (13:1–7). 'Authority' occurs five times in the Revised Standard Version of these verses. The subject is very topical for us since one of the facts of modern life is a revolt against authority of all kinds, and its breakdown in certain areas. Paul talks a great deal about authority. 'Let every person be subject to the governing authorities. For there is no authority except from God . . . ' The basic fact he wants to underline is that authority, as an idea, was invented by God. That's what he is saying in verse 1.

That doesn't mean that God is pleased with everybody who exercises authority. It does mean that God is the author of the idea. The Christian does not blindly praise authority however it is exercised, but he does recognise its origin. So his attitude to authority will be one of respect and submission, not just because it is a good thing for society but because it is our duty before God. Let me explain what I mean.

To deny authority is really to deny two fundamental things about man. One, his creatureliness; the other, his fallenness. God's authority over us evidences our creatureliness. He made us to live in such a way that we need His authority in our lives. It was true in man's unfallen state, and man was put into Eden with authoritative instructions on how to live aright. God's delegation of His authority in the civil, domestic and commercial spheres which you find in the giving of the Law and in so many other places in Scripture, is a hedge against our sinfulness, and the tendency within us to rebel against authority. It's these things which are being denied in the current revolt against established authority; that's one of the reasons why it is so important to have a truly biblical view of man. In the intellectual world, the libertarian repudiates all intellectual authority over man, except that which self-authenticates. In the social realm, even the permissive society is rejected by some people as a shade too paternalistic! Instead there is the alternative society, in which there is no authority and everybody is free to make up his own mind. They think it's a modern idea! Of course, it's commented on at the end of the Book of Judges, that 'every man did that which was right in his own eyes.' In such a society, for example, all censorship is abolished, even for the very young. And the implication is that man is not a creature, or that he is not a sinner.

Well, let me give you five propositions to sum up what I think the apostle is saying in these verses.

The first proposition is: *the ultimate authority, and the only universal and absolute one, is God* (verse 1). Ultimately all men will be answerable to God, which has already been implied in the last section of chapter 12. It's been laid down in Genesis 1 to 3 (man is a creature), and reinforced at Sinai in the giving of the Law. And it's visibly demonstrated, supremely, 'when every knee shall bow and every tongue confess that Jesus Christ is Lord.'

The second proposition is: *God delegates some of His authority.* He passes it on to certain people saying 'Use that, for Me.' Do you notice at the end of verse 1, that the authorities that exist 'have been instituted by God'? And also in verses 4 and 6. The principle extends to all proper spheres, including (it seems to me, from Scripture) to husbands in marriage, parents within the family, and masters within the servant/master relationship – however you interpret that for modern times. Let me say again, it doesn't imply that God is pleased with those who abuse authority given them.

Third, *to resist authority is to resist God* (verse 2). This is how Scripture teaches us to view rebellion against instituted authority; it is like rebellion against God.

Fourth, *such rebellion merits punishment* (verses 2 and 4). It seems to me inescapable to conclude this is so. Laws always have to be accompanied by penalties for breaking them. Clearly this biblical doctrine of punishment is neither primarily reformative ('Don't do it again') nor deterrent ('Let that be a lesson to others'), but retributive ('This is the just reward for your misdeeds').

The question obviously arises at this point: is all resistance to authority therefore forbidden? In our modern world that's an important question, especially in the international sphere. The exception is: when the governing authority commands us to disobey God. In verse 7 Paul urges, 'Pay all of them their dues' (a reflection of Jesus' words, 'Render to Caesar . . . '). But if Caesar demands the things that are God's, then the answer must be that of Peter in Acts 5: 'We ought to obey God, rather than men.' 'In certain circumstances,' wrote Sir Thomas Taylor, 'disobedience to the State may not only be a right, but a duty. This has been classical Christian doctrine ever since the apostle declared that they ought to obey God rather than men.'

We need to think some of these things through, however briefly. Does this mean that a Christian can support and engage in violent revolution? It's a real issue in many parts of the world today. I would suggest, on both biblical and theological grounds, that the answer is 'No'. On biblical grounds, I would want to point out that the only two instances of civil disobedience, in Acts 5 and Revelation 13, are concerned with a defence of the liberty to worship God. Paul, in 1 Timothy 2:2, urges us to pray for all in authority, with this in view. And I would want to point out that Jesus turned down the clamour of the masses to become a violent revolutionary, in John 6:15. He said that His kingship was not brought about by this means. On theological grounds I would want to point out further that sin is endemic in man's nature, not in his environment. The root of injustice is in the heart of men, and that's why so many revolutions end in disappointment and violence ends in despair.

Finally, we must recognise that *the institution of authority was meant by God for our greater good and the common well-being* (verses 3 and 4). Now you can't just restrict that to Christian governments, or even ones with Christian orientations, because in the Old Testament you find God speaking through Jeremiah to the people of Israel: 'Serve the King of Babylon, and live.' It meant going into captivity. But God sent them there, to serve the King of Babylon. We need to recognise that authority and freedom are not alternatives. Authority makes true freedom possible.

I want to say to young people: the alternative to authority is not liberty, but anarchy and then tyranny. That's what makes the current revolt against authority so alarming. The only place where true freedom is to be found is in bondage to Jesus Christ and total submission to the authority of His lordship. And that involves submission to the authority of His word, which bids us to be submitted to the governing authority. And this is the Christian way of life.

3. Verses 8–10: the obligation of Christian love to our neighbour

Let me now draw your attention to how Paul underlines this whole concept of obligation in relation to love. Notice he moves from verse 7, the paying of what is due, to verse 8, the obligation of love. Notice how many times the word 'due' appears in verse 7; he is speaking there about the whole realm of duty. You have a duty, he says, to discharge these obligations. But even more binding is the duty of love. The idea of love being an obligation or duty is one that many people find hard to accept. How can I be under obligation to love anybody? Two misunderstandings prompt this, I think. The first is a misunderstanding of the nature of Christian love. We tend to think of it – do we not? – as a kind of feeling, a sort of afflatus come upon us, which we are incapable of calling up or dismissing. But Christian love in the New Testament is regarding and dealing with people as God has regarded and dealt with us; it has a moral content. It is not (in John Stott's excellent contrast) the victim of our emotions, but the servant of our will.

The other misunderstanding is of the whole place of duty in the Christian life. May I say that I think we as evangelicals are weak in this whole area of duty and obligation. We quote 'Render unto Caesar the things that are Caesar's' – and we stop there. But Jesus didn't! 'And render unto God the things that are God's.' In other words, just as you have a duty to pay your taxes, you have an obligation to God to love your neighbour. Now you don't pay your taxes according to your emotional feelings, but we so often imagine that that's the way we are called to live the Christian life. But, for example, prayer is a duty. 'Men ought always to pray, and not to faint.' We are called on by God to pray. Samuel said, 'God forbid that I should sin against the Lord in ceasing to pray for you.'

We need to learn this place of duty. Notice, Paul does not say (verses 8–10) that law is love, or that love replaces law. He says, 'Love fulfils the law.' 'If you love me,' said Jesus, 'keep My commandments.' Love will prevent us breaking the law, says Paul, mentioning four specific areas at the end of verse 9. You will see there that this is the kind of love which puts our neighbour in place of ourself.

4. Verses 11–14: the obligations deriving from the coming day of the Lord

They are obligations of holiness of life. Paul is, as it were, like the town crier, calling on men to recognise what the hour is. The great day is coming.

These two chapters, 12 and 13, taken together begin and end with an exhortation, an appeal. The first, as we have seen, is in 12:1–2, based on the display of God's mercy in Jesus Christ. Something that lay in the past, for these Christians at Rome. And the appeal there is to consecrate our bodies as a living sacrifice to Him.

Now this closing appeal at the end of chapter 13 is based on something that lies ahead of them, the display of God's full glory in salvation when the day dawns for Christ's appearing. The appeal is to holy living, the casting off of the works of darkness, the putting on of the armour of light. It's significant that here as elsewhere in Scripture both the appearings of the Lord Jesus Christ are used as incentives to holiness. 'Our salvation is nearer than when we believed.' You notice, the apostle speaks of salvation in the broader sense that we mentioned in our previous study. It's not something finished with, in the here and now. We have of course received full salvation in Jesus Christ, but, there is something infinitely more that God has yet to do for us. That's the glorious thing about being a child of God! The best is yet to be. The dawn is yet to break. The glory is yet to come.

That day is the day to which we, and the whole creation, and the whole universe, are moving. The climax of the ages will come on that day. We belong to that age, says Paul. That's where you have your roots. That's where your true inheritance is; that's where your real life is. It's in the coming King. You'll see what salvation is all about, and the world will see it, when He appears in His infinite glory. And He will be admired by all them that believe.

But, you see, that's the point. That day is hastening on. And the great danger, my beloved, is that we grow careless. It's so easy for us to slumber, to get careless about the glory of God, the health of our soul, the quality of our Christian testimony, and the state of a man without Christ. Slumbering . . . And the apostle says, 'The night is far spent, the day is at hand: let us therefore cast off the works of darkness, and let us put on the armour of light.' You see the contrast: works of darkness – armour of light. These bedfellows are very significant. The works of darkness are expounded in verse 13. The armour speaks of the fact that in these last days as the dawn is about to break, the battle will grow no less fierce. Put on the armour. What is it? It's expounded in verse 14. It isn't just the opposite moral quality to the degrading works of darkness. The armour of light is put on the Lord Jesus Christ. It is nothing less than the moral glory and the moral beauty of our Lord Jesus that we are to be wearing, as we move towards the day of His coming.

3. Romans 14:1–23

The theme of chapter 14 is *the Christian way of life in relation to our attitudes to others over doubtful things*. It is in a sense a new theme, though the apostle is still working out the implications for Christian behaviour of a consecrated body, a renewed mind, and a transformed character. And the theme of chapter 14 flows on from the obligation of Christian love which concerns Paul in 13:8. So much of chapters 12 and 13 dealt with various relationships which truly test our consecration to God; but here Paul turns to a relationship which exists within the fellowship of the church between true believers. Not now in the alien world, but in the church. Our relationship with other Christians, with whom we differ over non-essentials. I think that's something of great relevance to the Christian church today.

What Paul is talking about in verses 1–3 is not just a remote situation, but one that exists in almost every Christian fellowship in every generation. Among fellow Christians there will always be differences of opinion. The danger is that these areas of difference will become like areas of dry tinder into which the devil just loves to throw a match. And we are not unfamiliar with the blazing fires that result. So we need to learn from God how to relate to those with whom we differ. And I would like us to have our thinking directed into three vital questions which we need to ask of this somewhat difficult chapter.

1. What are these doubtful issues, of which the apostle speaks?

Perhaps I can begin by clarifying what they are not. Note the word 'doubtful'. Paul is not referring to those who differ over the truth of the gospel, which is never referred to as 'doubtful' in the New Testament. Tolerance and a welcome, which Paul urges us to give to those with different opinions, are the very reverse of what he extends to those who differ over the centralities of the gospel. Galatians 1:9, 'If any man preach any other gospel than that which we have preached unto you, let him be anathema.' He is intolerant and unwelcoming to any distortion of the gospel.

Nor is he speaking of a difference of opinion over matters of Christian behaviour where clear-cut commands from God exist; that is, in matters of ordinary morality, or Christian duty. For such issues there is no room for debate. Some things are not negotiable; because one thing is right, and another is wrong. That's important to grasp in an age which is intolerant of dogmatism, and television programmes (especially religious ones, I may add) give assent to two diametrically opposed views.

No, Paul is not advocating a mushy tolerance about everything with convictions about nothing. He is dealing not with centralities but with marginal issues. What he be anxious to avoid is not true spiritual discernment, but what carping critical spirit which loves an argument – especially over trivia. And that has tended to be an evangelical phenomenon.

What are these marginal issues? They seem to be of two kinds. *Matters of personal behaviour,* particularly related to *special diets* (verse 2); and *matters of church observance*, particularly related to *special days* (verse 5). These are areas where Scripture is either silent or not dogmatic – areas of speculation rather than revelation.

Special diets. One context of this is probably Jewish dietary laws. Not Old Testament dietary laws – that's a different thing. They didn't forbid meat eating in general. But the church historian Josephus tells us that some Jews in Rome followed a strict vegetarian diet. It was a Jewish tradition rather than an Old Testament law. Another possibility is that some of these people were influenced by the Essene sect, of which you will have heard because the Dead Sea Scrolls came from them. Some of the Essenes had longstanding traditional laws about meat-eating.

A second context would perhaps be the offering of meat to idols. Much butcher's meat in those days would have been so offered, and it was almost impossible to tell if what you were eating had been offered to idols. Now some people would have said, 'So what? Christ has freed us from bondage, and these idols are dead figures anyway.' Others, on the other hand, would have said, 'How can we possibly eat this meat? We will rather be vegetarians.'

Special days. The issue seems to have been the ceremonial holy days of the levitical institution. Some felt that they should continue to keep the solemn days and festivals and other special days; I think it's important to say here that Paul can hardly be referring to the Christian Lord's day, for the Sabbath principle belongs to the moral law in the decalogue, not the ceremonial law. Not only so, but it is a creation ordinance preceding the moral law. In the New Testament it is perpetual recurring memorial to Jesus' resurrection: the early church gathered to break bread on that day (Acts 20:7). So I suggest that Paul is instead referring to the high days and holy days, because otherwise, he would be calling somebody who was concerned to keep the moral law, the weaker brother.

I must add that I think Paul *is* referring here to Sabbatarianism in some of its odder forms. The modern equivalent might for instance be special days like Good Friday. You will nowhere in Scripture find Good Friday to be a special day for Christians to observe; yet I have a friend who is a minister who will *never* marry somebody on Good Friday – he regards it as a very special day. This may be a particular issue. And I suppose, if you want an example that brings the two questions of diets and days together, it might be the man who will not eat meat on Friday.

But Paul's principle applies to all kinds of marginal issues, where, I say again, Scripture is silent and tradition is vocal, whether it be national, ecclesiastical, cultural or family traditions. They all affect us deeply, some of them become dogma inadvertently, and that's one of the grave dangers of the situation.

There are cultural backgrounds as well. In Indonesia, in Java, I went into a pastors' conference session, and could hardly see any of the men – godly men mightily used in Indonesia – because they were all smoking. Well, you see, it was from the Dutch cultural tradition which was part of their lives. I didn't think it was helpful to them, but it was a cultural factor. There are many less important things than these that have become part of the fibre of our lives. And one of the important themes of chapter 14 is: getting the really important things put first.

2. Who are the people to whom Paul refers?

We can answer this more briefly. They're described in 14:1 as 'the weak'. And in 15:1, 'We who are strong ought to bear with the failings of the weak.' The weak may be over-scrupulous Christians from a Jewish background on one hand; and on the other, Gentile converts. What we know for sure is that the weak brother (and here may be a surprise for you) is the one who has most scruples and is most tender in his conscience about all these do's and don'ts. We tend to think, don't we, that the man who won't do this or that, and has scruples about almost every detail of these cultural matters, is the strong Christian. But Paul says he is the weak one (verse 2). The temptation is to get caught up in the details of such issues as these, become distracted from the things that are central, and be disabled for serving God in the things which really do matter.

3. What is the counsel that the apostle gives?

This is our main theme in this study. What is the Christian way of life in these circumstances? Well, Paul lays down seven basic and important principles, of very wide application over doubtful issues.

The first is this: *welcome those whom God welcomes* (verses 1 and 3, and 15:7). You will notice the irony in the last part of verse 3. Here are some believers holding such a brother at arm's length, being cold towards him, refusing him fellowship and membership within the church or, more likely, just refusing to open their hearts to him totally without reservation – to show him true, warm, generous Christian love and welcome. Because he doesn't dot all their ecclesiastical i's and stroke their t's exactly as they do! Yet God has welcomed him; Christ has welcomed him; and the problem is therefore that you're out of sorts with God and His son, because you're holding back.

Now here's the principle, and I quote to you the words of that great commentator on Romans, Charles Hodge: 'If God has not made it a barrier to communion with Him, we dare not make it a barrier to fellowship with us.' It's not just a question, of being 'holier-than-thou'.

It's a question of being 'holier-than-God'.

The welcome has two qualifications. Verse 1, 'but not for disputes over opinions'. Don't welcome him in just to eat him up. Do not make the church of God a place for arguments about stupidities and trivialities. And the second qualification is: this is not to be a cold, grudging welcome which exemplifies the warmth and depth and genuineness of the love of God in Jesus Christ.

The second principle is: *avoid either judging or despising others* (verses 3 and 4). There are two tendencies, further amplified in verses 10 to 13. The weak brother tends to sit in judgement on the strong, who doesn't have such scruples as himself. It is easy, as James Denny pointed out, to lapse from scrupulousness about one's own conduct to pharisaism about that of others. The strong brother, on the other hand, tends to despise the weak brother, who in his eyes is just a pathetic crank.

Behind both attitudes is the ugly spirit of which Jesus warned in Matthew 7 (as I've said, Romans 12 to 14 and the Sermon on the Mount have a great deal in common); the spirit of censorious criticism, which Paul condemns in verse 10.

Paul states three things that are wrong about this spirit which so often arises from these marginal matters, about which Scripture is not dogmatic. In verse 3 he says it is *judgement on the wrong issues.* It is judgement of trivia, and it's significant that in Matthew 7 this is what Jesus puts his finger on. 'Why do you say to your brother, "Let me take the speck out of your eye"?' A speck is something you have to look for consciously. It's minutiae, trivia. It's judgement by shibboleth. You remember the story in Judges 12 where that word is found. Look it up. Paul is saying that here we have judgement on the basis of shibboleth. So much of our judging and despising of others is on the basis of whether we can pronounce our shibboleth. That's one of the applications of verse 17.

But the other major error of this judgement is that it

is *judgement by the wrong people*. Look at verses 4 and 10. Verse 4 implies that judging your brother is like interfering in the domestic affairs of someone else's family. The standard that will be applied to your brother is the standard his own master sets – and his own master is Christ. And He will not judge on the basis of trivia. If we judge we condemn one whom the Lord has made to stand (verse 4). So the real controversy is not between you and your brother, but between you and his Lord.

Verses 10 to 12 take this a stage further and here Paul says that it is *judgement at the wrong time*. We are anticipating the judgement seat of God. At that judgement seat we shall all have to give an account of ourselves. That means our censorious word and our despising spirit will be judged before God. It is not for my brother's scruples or absence of them that I will have to answer, but my own.

Here is the third principle: *think things through for yourself* (verse 5). It's simply an extension of Paul's appeal in 12:1–2, for conduct which springs from a renewed mind. Christian conduct is not a case of an endless list of do's and don'ts. It is not to be moulded by taboos and prejudices. It is to be decided by gaining the mind of Christ on every issue, thinking through them with a consecrated, biblical mind.

Now this is of great importance. There is a mindlessness about many supposedly Christian attitudes which can lead you away from Christian liberty in two directions. On one hand it can lead you to licence – because 'everybody's doing it'. I'm amazed at the number of Christians who say, 'Of course all Christians are doing this, or that, nowadays.' The answer is, 'So what?' Or, it can lead you into legalism, because *nobody's* doing it, in your circle. Paul says, be fully convinced in your own mind. He is not interested in a mere set of rules for outward conformity. He is interested in the renewal of Christian character through renewing of the mind. This is what God has given us His word for, to enable us to think things through with the mind of Christ. It furnishes us with 'just principles to direct our conduct', as John Newton said. This is one of the vital reasons for being under a consistent ministry of the word of God, because God shapes our minds and forms our thinking, so that we think things through with the mind of God.

This is not to say that there are no standards, that one man's opinion is as good as another's. That's not what Paul is saying. The standards are the standards by which our judgement is to be formed: the authority of Scripture and the lordship of Christ. Which leads me to the fourth principle.

The fourth principle is: *live under the lordship of Christ* (verses 6 to 9). Again and again, it is honouring the Lord, and living to the Lord, of which Paul speaks, until the great climax in verse 9. Our liberty is to be controlled by Christ's lordship. You will notice, *we* do not make Jesus Lord. God the Father has already done this, it is the reward for Jesus' humiliation. This lordship he has achieved by His death and His resurrection. If I were to leave the last word of verse 9 blank, and say to you, 'To this end Christ died and lived again, that He might be — ' – I'm sure almost all of you would say, 'Saviour'. But Paul says, 'Lord'. It has been said that it's possible to have Jesus as your Saviour but not as your Lord – 'I didn't accept Him as Lord when I accepted Him first as Saviour.' But I want to say to you, the New Testament knows nothing of that strange phenomenon! There is only one Jesus Christ, who is both Lord and Saviour.

We *acknowledge* His lordship. It is a fact before we discover it. He has the right to rule over our lives. From verse 6 onwards, this touches almost every area Paul is dealing with. The direction of the whole of life is to be toward the lordship of Jesus.

This is the freedom that the gospel brings; freedom to obey Him whose service is perfect. As Gifford has written, 'If it should seem irksome to bow so completely to the lordship of Christ, let us remind ourselves it is not a philosophy or an abstraction, far less a tyrant, to whom we give homage, but the greatest lover in the whole universe.'

The fact of my liberty is controlled and defined by the fact of Christ's lordship.

The fifth principle: *let liberty be controlled by love.* From verse 13, the apostle urges us that the Christian way of life in relation to those with whom we differ over unimportant issues is to be marked not by condemnation of them but by consideration of them. There is a play of meanings in verse 13, for the word 'judge'. Paul juxtaposes a prohibition of judgement by condemnation, with a command to apply our judgement of reason to avoid giving offence. The word for 'hindrance' really means the springing of a trap – a death trap, suggests Lenski. So we are to resolve never to be the cause of hurt or harm to our brother, but to be sensitive by God's grace to what will help him and what will hinder him.

This is because as Christians we live under the law of liberty and we live under the law of love. We need to be able to hold these two things together in all our relationships with other people, particularly in this area. Freedom is what Christ has liberated us for, from all foolish forms of bondage. Martin Luther stated: 'The Christian is a most free lord of all, subject to none.' But then we must add, that the Christian is under the law of love. In verse 14 Paul joins the two together. In Galatians 5:13 Paul makes the same point, and, to the similarly-troubled Corinthians, he wrote: 'All things are lawful for me, but all things are not expedient.'

So this is how it works out. The application of the law of love does not mean that we cease to be free. But it does mean that if we walk in love as well as in liberty we shall be preserved from using our liberty to indulge our selfishness; it all comes down to the issue of whether I am living on the basis of self-indulgence, or love. The Christian has the great privilege of surrendering his rights to the Lord. We're strong on our 'rights' in this generation. I keep hearing the phrase on radio and television. But we are weak on our duties. Many people quote the Martin Luther quotation I have just given you, but few go on to quote what he went on to say: 'The Christian man is also a most dutiful servant of all, subject to all.'

In verse 15 there's a compelling reason given us for the exercise of this brotherly love and consideration. Your brother is one for whom Christ died. Paul uses exactly the same argument and phrase in 1 Corinthians 8:11. How different, he emphasises here, the careless hurtful attitudes we have to fellow believers, to the attitude Christ has to them! He loved them to the extent of dying to save them. There's an obvious contrast between the infinite sacrifice He made for this brother, and the trivial sacrifice I am unwilling to make for him. It will be expounded in chapter 15, but we should notice the point here in passing.

Now here's the sixth element. *Let the things that matter to God be the things that matter to you.* That's the message of verse 17. Paul's real worry is the worry that one would have in the same situation at the present time. So much time, mental energy and resources has been expended on trivia, marginal issues. The evangelical church is brilliant at doing this. I saw an advertisement for an American church which said: 'We are a premillenial, dispensationalist, pre-tribulation, single rapture church and welcome all who are one with us in Christ.' We do it, you see. We have these things which are marginal, and they become central. Do you live and speak, asks Paul, as if the marginal issues of Christian living and practices and ecclesiastical tradition were the central things? They are not! Verse 17; the great concerns of the church are the spiritual blessings of the gospel. And *they* are the things that we are to get steamed up about. Righteousness –

that inward quality of life in relationship to ourselves. Peace – that quality of life in relation to others. Joy – that quality of life in relation to God. These are the things that matter, and these priorities will shape our attitude to the church (verse 19) and to the work of God (verse 20).

The last strand of Paul's counsel is very simple: *if in doubt, don't!* (verses 22 and 23). If you have a clear conscience, says Paul, then don't surrender your liberty. But don't brandish it – let it be between you and God. On the other hand, if the weak brother disregards his convictions for any other reason than the pressure of conviction, then he is sinning against God, because he doesn't really believe that what he is doing is right. If you have doubts about a course of action, don't do it; because you cannot act in faith. Act on principle, says Paul, never on expediency.

And the great principle is the principle of faith, and with this we finish. But faith, in Scripture, cannot be separated from obedience. It is faith in Jesus as Lord. And there are so many areas, in which the doctrine of the lordship of Christ is the key doctrine in this whole realm of Christian living. For our relationship with Him, with one another and with the world. It is the supreme banner under which we are to live; the banner of the absolute, universal, all-embracing lordship of Jesus.

4. Romans 15:1–13

It's frequently said that Paul, at the beginning of Romans 15, is simply concluding the treatment of the question of doubtful things, which is the subject of chapter 14. But that subject is only touched on in 15:1, and it is touched on in order to lead into a much broader field of teaching. The general theme is a call for life focused on others rather than ourselves. This theme occupies the first thirteen verses of chapter 15, after which Paul turns to more personal, domestic matters, at the end of the epistle.

Verse 1 is the link, with its emphasis on the duty of the strong in relation to the weak. Here Paul is not merely counselling patience with the infirmities of the weak and a good humoured tolerance of their foibles; he is urging the strong to bear the infirmities of the weak in the sense of bearing and supporting those burdens. And this is a great principle for every such relationship in any fellowship, however 'strength' and 'weakness' are to be interpreted. At the beginning of Galatians 6 you find that same principle, because the word 'bear' does not mean just 'tolerate'. It means to carry a load for someone. It's the rather lovely picture of those who are stronger within the fellowship showing such loving care for the weaker ones that they say, 'Now that's not a burden you should be carrying, let me get under it with you.' That sort of attitude would solve so many of our problems. In Galatians 6:2, Paul shows that this burden-sharing is part of the law of Christ. It is an example of the selfless life focused on others for the glory of God, of which passage has much to say.

That is the alternative lifestyle and the alternative society which our Lord Jesus is building, in the increasingly self-centred world in which we live. We are called to be members of that alternative society and to live that self-giving lifestyle for the sake of others, living (verse 1) not to please ourselves but to please our neighbour for his good.

This is not an inconsistent Pauline plea, that we should indulge in what he elsewhere condemns as 'men-pleasing', as for example in Galatians 1:10 and Ephesians 6:6. The point, rather, is that there is more to be considered than the relative places of God and self in the soul. And I think that this is a very important thing to grasp. You see, a 'pure motive', to please the Lord in the exercise of our Christian liberty, is not enough. It's a question of putting one's fellow-Christian above oneself also. Sometimes this is the real test. Let me put it to you in the words of John in 1 John 4:20: 'He who does not love his brother whom he has seen, how can he love God whom he has not seen?'

Now Paul further defines the purity of this neighbour love of which he speaks in verse 2, by adding two qualifying phrases: 'Let each of us please his neighbour *for his good, to edify him.*' True neighbour love says, 'I desire God's highest good for you.' It needs guidelines, you notice. It is directed by a desire for God's glory in their lives for their good and to edify, to build them up, in Him. My whole heart is to be set on whatever will build my brother up in Christ. I am to shun whatever will draw him away from Christ, whatever will put a stumbling block in his way.

In verse 3, Paul cites the perfect example of this quality of selfless living: Jesus Christ. Another situation which comes to mind is in Philippians 2:5, where there is disagreement and self-seeking among some of the people in the Philippian church. And again Paul sets the example of Jesus before them; he uses the highest doctrine to commend the humblest duty. That, of course, is the great purpose of these glorious doctrines of the faith. It is doctrine which produces character, in the economy of God. That's why it is important that we are not lazy or superficial in our understanding of the great truths of the word of God. They are character-forming. The infinite selflessness of our Lord Jesus is therefore not only the *means of our justification,* it is the *pattern of our sanctification.*

And there has never been a more costly refusal to indulge self-interest. Paul finds a striking example of it in the psalm he quotes in verse 3. From Psalm 69, 'The reproaches of those who reproached Thee have fallen on me.' Remember Christ . . . His self-denial was of infinite proportion, says Paul, compared with the trivial irritation you are bearing. If Christ had pleased Himself and clung to the privileges which were His, where would we have been?

There is a pattern here which is the key to fruitfulness both in life and in service to God. The pattern is the pattern of dying to self and living to God. Our Saviour's death and resurrection, in that they were redemptive, are unique. But, as Jesus illustrates in John 12:24, they are a pattern for us also. Here is the problem, so often, in our refusal to be like Jesus. It centres upon a refusal of self to die.

The call of God is a call to die. Paul knew about that, in the thousand deaths that he was called to die. Out of those deaths, the fruitfulness of his ministry sprang.

The quotation from Psalm 69 leads Paul to draw a more general lesson in verse 4. What he is speaking of in this verse is the relevance of Scripture. You get another example in 1 Corinthians 10, when, after a great account of the history of Israel, Paul says: 'Now these things happened to them as a warning, but they were written down for our instruction.' It is the instruction necessary for the fulfilment of our vocation in the will of God. So, when we are summoned, at the beginning of this section of Romans, into the will of God in all its fullness, that by the presentation of our bodies and the renewing of our minds and the transforming of our character, we might prove the will of God – how are we to do this? Well, says the apostle, the instruction is from the word of God. You cannot just live this Christian way of life to which these chapters summon us, without constantly being under the ministry of the Scriptures. Seeking to live the Christian way of life divorced from that leads eventually to despair.

'That . . . we might have hope' – you see, the demands of Scripture and the duties of the Christian life could so easily lead us into a spirit of hopelessness. How can we be delivered from that spirit? Well, he says in verse 4, there are two things we need: 'steadfastness' – that's perseverance and 'encouragement'.

Look at these words in verse 4. 'Perseverance'. It's the same word you find at the beginning of Hebrews 12, for example. We need perseverance, we need to 'keep on'. This word is one of the key words of Christian living. In classical Greek it's normally found either in a military context, describing the man who does not flee the field of battle but keeping on to the end, or in the context of athletics, describing, as in Hebrews 12, the runner in a race. This is the picture in Hebrews. It's the quality Paul longs for. Where do you find it? he asks. You find it in Scripture; God ministers it to us through the Scriptures.

'Encouragement' is the same word as is used for the Holy Spirit in John 14 – the 'Paraclete', the one 'called alongside'. This is what Jesus saw the disciples were going to need. The Holy Spirit was going to come and be the encourager, to hold the burden up when it became too heavy, to take them on to the end.

The significant thing is this. These two words appear both in verses 4 and 5; the same words. In verse 4, they come from the Scripture; in verse 5, they come from God. The point is obvious. Perseverance and encouragement come from God. They are gifts to His children. But, and here is the point, the vessel in which God bears these blessings to His people is holy Scripture. This, He has decreed, is how He will minister perseverance and encouragement to us, so that we might live hopefully. And that's why we need to be absorbing God's word into our lives. So often, discouragement and hopelessness have their roots in a neglect of God's word. Through the Scriptures we come to know God in all His fullness. This is where we get in touch with His grace and sufficiency, His might and power, truth and glory. That's what the Bible is. It's the place where we come to know God. And that's the great need of our lives. With such a God as we have been discovering in His word, how shall we faint or fear?

But note also in verse 5 that God does not only keep His servants persevering and encouraged by the instruction of Scripture. He also uses the intercession of the saints. Verse 5 is not merely a wish. It is the expression of a prayer. Have you noticed how easily Paul in his epistles can move from exhortation to intercession? And here he is crying to the Lord for these Roman Christians, that they might live in harmony with each other, to the glory of the God and Father of our Lord Jesus Christ. That's another way in which people may be kept going and be saved from discouragement. Praying was one of Paul's great ministries.

What does Paul pray for? He prays first for harmony in their fellowship. The phrase 'in accord with Christ Jesus' is literally 'to be minding the same things according to Christ Jesus' – very reminiscent of the similar phrase in Philippians 2:5. Both there and in this chapter Paul is speaking of the harmony that derives from humility in accordance with Jesus' self-humbling. Paul prays that they might have a harmony that is in accordance with the mind of Jesus, and there is no true Christian harmony to be got any other way.

That harmony in the fellowship produces the other thing Paul prays for, which is unity in worship – 'together . . . with one voice' (verse 6). I'm sure that here Paul is speaking about the common public worship, and there is much to learn from what he has to say.

We learn that true worship derives from the spiritual condition of God's people, by and large. That's why the secret of worship is not to be found in forms, whether old or new. It's to be found in being united by a common desire to glorify God through Jesus Christ. And the link with what has gone before is the example of the Lord Jesus, on the one hand abasing Himself, and on the other, glorifying the Father. That's significant, isn't it? So, after all these chapters about Christian character, Paul turns to speak about the kind of fellowship that together, with one voice, glorifies the God and Father of the Lord Jesus Christ.

Have you ever noticed what the people of God in heaven are doing at the throne of God, in the Book of Revelation? They are seeking to exalt God to the highest glory, and to humble themselves. You remember Elijah on Carmel, crying to God for rain? He is bowing down with his face to the ground and his head between his knees. You try that some time! The significance of it is that he can't get any lower than that. That's the significance of it. And that's how they're worshipping in heaven. Read Revelation 7. That's real worship; but you don't get that from forms. It comes out of what God's grace has done in a man's character. He longs for the glory of God with all his being. It is the burning passion of his life. He longs to get as low as he can, to humble himself under God's mighty hand. And *that's* where God's people are worshipping.

It happens in revival. And oh, God knows how we need this spirit of worship.

Now at the beginning of the second half of this passage, the apostle is widening the appeal not only to include the strong and the weak, but to include every kind of divisiveness which could arise in the church. Once again, Christ's example is normative. 'Welcome one another, therefore as Christ has welcomed you, for the glory of God.' It's not just an official welcome. It is a loving, costly giving of ourselves without stint to one another. That is what true Christian fellowship means. There are many practical implications of this. We need to ask, is this how fellowship really is experienced in our churches? I have seen lonely, introverted people, shy and perhaps unattractive, excluded by a phalanx of fellowship; by a group of Christians all sharing the good things they enjoy together, leaving the lonely Christians outside. True fellowship never springs from a life of self-pleasing, but from the heart of Jesus and His self-giving love.

If we are to follow Jesus' pattern, we are also to follow His motive; verse 7, ' . . . for the glory of God.' Everything that Jesus did focused on that. Indeed throughout the Scriptures everything done by the Godhead conspires to that end. Have you ever thought of this? It was the design of the Father in creation. It was the design of the Son in the redemption of His people. And, says Paul, 'We are being changed into the same image from glory into glory even as by the Spirit of God.' God's great purpose is that everything might conspire to this end. There is nothing beyond this for the child of God. The glory of God is everything.

From verse 8, Paul elaborates on just how extensive Christ's welcome is. If the theme of verse 6 was worship, and the theme of verse 7 was fellowship, then the theme of verse 8 is the church's third great activity – mission. '. . . In order that the Gentiles might glorify God for His mercy.' Again it is the nature of Christ's service who is a pattern for ours.

We must go rather quickly through these verses; I hope you will study them at your leisure. Paul is saying, from verse 8 onwards, that Christ came to the Jews for the Gentiles. This was the purpose and plan of God in sending a Saviour. In other words, the salvation of the Gentiles was not an afterthought of God. It was this missionary vision and vocation that Christ had when He came into this world. Paul expounds this doctrine of mission in four stages.

First: *Christ became a servant* (verse 8). That's the basis of it. And it was not merely a title, it was an office He bore – compare again Philippians 2:7. That position is one we should adopt to each other. We are called to service and servanthood, because Christ became a servant. That's true of every one of us who are Christians.

Second: *He was sent to the Jews.* 'I am not come,' said Jesus to the Canaanite woman, 'except to the lost house of Israel.' Now there is a sense of this compulsion upon Jesus in His ministry, that He had been sent specifically to the Jews. But more than that,

Third: *He was sent in the interests of God's covenant with Abraham.* It's an enormously important statement: '. . . in order to confirm the promises given to the patriarchs'. There is a sense in which you cannot understand the meaning of Jesus' coming, apart from this. He came as a fulfilment of God's covenant promise to Abraham, which was sealed by circumcision – hence the reference in verse 8 to circumcision. There is a direct line, which Matthew points to in his genealogy, from Abraham to Bethlehem. At Bethlehem, God was mindful of His covenant. This is what they were singing about when Jesus was born. In Christ God is fulfilling His promise to Abraham. That's where the mercies of God reach back to.

And fourth: *He came ultimately in the interests of the salvation of the Gentiles* (verse 9). The Jew is reminded that (as Moule puts it), 'the promise of salvation, while given wholly through the Jew, was not given wholly for him.' That was what Simeon was singing about in the temple: 'A light, for revelation to the Gentiles.' He gave the charter for missionary vocation there. That's what it is.

And from verse 9 Paul reinforces this missionary vision with extensive quotations from Scripture (verses 9 to 12). It's not without significance that he quotes from the three sections of the Hebrew Bible – the Law, the Prophets, and the Writings. Paul, you see, is urging on his people that the doctrine of mission is a Christian doctrine. The God of the Bible is not narrowly preoccupied either with our own little group or our own little nation. He is not the God of the Jews only but the Gentiles also. And God's design was that the Gentiles should know His name, belong to His people, praise Him for His grace, and acknowledge His lordship.

That's *the biblical basis for mission,* beloved. Paul is saying that the God of the Bible is a missionary God; the Christ of the gospel is a missionary Saviour: that the Old Testament is a missionary book: and that the church is meant to be a missionary church. And that means a missionary obligation, laid on every church. Why? Well, Paul gives us here not just the biblical basis for the mission, but *the biblical motive for mission*, and it's in verse 9: ' . . . in order that the Gentiles might glorify God for His mercy.' Here again, the only ultimate motive is the glory of God. It applies like this. If I have shared in any real way in God's zeal and jealousy for His own glory, then what will move me most will be that there may be an area of the world, or a people, in whose lives God is being robbed of His glory. That's the great motive of mission. Does it matter to you that God is being robbed of His glory? Does it matter to you the way it mattered to Paul in Athens, when he saw the sophisticated Athenians giving themselves to idol worship? We read that Paul was provoked in his spirit. Do you know what that means? It is the same word that is used in medical Greek for a heart attack. Does it matter to you, all you that pass by?

There is the biblical motive for mission. The apostle provides us with our closing prayer in verse 13: 'May the God of hope fill you with all joy and peace in believing, so that by the power of the Holy Spirit you may abound in hope.'

How shall we live this Christian way of life? How shall we go into this sick world of ours and live like this, as the apostle has been describing to us? The answer is in that little phrase, 'by the power of the Holy Spirit'. Oh, may God grant us an access to that power, for the glorifying of His name in the world, and for the healing of the nations.

Notes

Notes

Notes

Notes

Notes

Notes

THE ADDRESSES

DO YOU BELIEVE IN GOD?

by Rev. Michael Baughen

Psalm 63

I've come to love the Psalms more and more, for their honesty and their constant inspiration. Psalm 63 expresses a faith in the living God, unshaken in adversity. I bring this psalm to you because I believe that in the foundation of many Christian lives there is a fundamental fault. It's one we're not aware of until tragedy, bereavement, suffering, trouble, some sort of testing hits us; then the fault is revealed. It springs from our 'pre-Christian' days, when we tended to think of God as a sort of genie of the lamp, there to do our will. If we prayed at all it was for our son to be safe, our husband to be delivered from troubles, for us to pass our exams or things of that kind. God was there, we prayed. You remember saying it, don't you, before you were a Christian? – 'I pray.' And we did, of a kind.

Of course we did not bother when everything was all right, only when we were in trouble. But then we became a Christian, and came to believe in the Lord Jesus Christ as our personal Saviour. It was a wonderful experience, a slow or perhaps a sudden one; and we came to grasp at the very roots of our being, that Jesus Christ bore our sin upon the cross and we are saved entirely because of Him. Yes, there is no doubt about it, we have come to believe in Jesus Christ, in saving faith.

But, I ask you, have you come to believe in God? Has that fundamental fault ever been corrected? Have you come to terms with believing in God? Or is God just there, to do what you want? So that when the stress comes, the break happens.

Now this Psalmist is going through an experience of suffering. He speaks of the dry and thirsty land, the desert, and his need both in body and soul. Here is a man passing through a difficult time, and here we find a man who has learnt the secret of believing in God.

Firstly, he is believing in *the centrality of God.* Let's get it clear. Who does the world revolve around? It revolves around God, but to many of us, it revolves around ourselves. That's what we thought before we were Christians, and many of us still do even though we are Christians. There are 4,000,000,000 people living on this earth, and you are just one of them. Does the world revolve around you? There are millions of people who are members of the world-wide church of Jesus Christ, and you are just one of them. Does the church revolve around you? 'No,' we say. 'Of course not! The world revolves around God and the church is submitted to its Head, Jesus Christ.' Yet, even though we know that, it constantly seems to get at Christians that underneath they still believe that they are the centre.

Well, here the Psalmist is the other way round: 'O God, You are my God.' In Psalm 46 you will remember the Psalmist says 'though the earth trembles and the mountains shake' – though the whole world seems to be going to bits around us, yet be still and know that God is God. The earth still trembles, the mountains are still shaking – it's not going away – but in the midst of it you can be still and know God is God. It's a faith that separates circumstances from God, to be in the midst of problems and yet at peace with the living God. That's the faith that breaks through. It has God at the centre.

You will be well aware of the wonderful passage in Hebrews 11 where the writer talks about the sort of faith which we are discussing here. 'Without faith,' he says (11:6), 'it is impossible to please God.' Then he spells out four different kinds of faith. There's the *loving, adoration faith* demonstrated by Abel bringing his best to God – the faith that lifts our hearts to praise Him. There's *exploit faith,* as I call it, that carried men like Noah, Abraham, and Moses. I love this faith, being involved in it, thrilled to go out into the unknown and test God and prove Him wonderfully faithful. It's exciting, they make films about it! Thirdly, *deliverance faith;* 11:33–35. This is when the mouths of the lions are stopped and people escape the sword and are raised from the dead. We've got endless paperbacks about that kind of faith – nothing wrong about it, it's marvellous to be involved in. It's part of Christian experience, a kind of faith. But there is a fourth kind of faith in Hebrews 11 which you don't hear so much about. Listen. 'By faith,' (11:36) 'they suffered mocking; scourging; chains . . . of whom the world was not worthy.'

'By faith'? Yes. Deliverance? No. No great exploit; destitution, death, suffering. Isn't that the greatest faith of all? That lays hold of the living God, when there is no break in the clouds? Isn't it so, that some of the greatest Christians you've ever known are people who've gone through suffering and glorified God? There is a faith that lays hold of God even in disaster. The ability to say 'God, I love You, I rejoice in You,' even in the midst of what humanly speaking is disaster is fantastic. Well, that's what the Psalmist is saying. 'O God, you are my God' – even though I'm going through this experience. It's the centrality of God.

Then look down to verse 2. He is sustained because he has grasped also *the power and the glory of God.* He's a great sanctuary man! You remember Psalm 73, when the Psalmist is fed up with the way evil prospers and the wicked get on well and those who do good don't seem to; then, when he goes into the sanctuary, in Psalm 73, he gets the perspective sorted out and comes out saying, 'Whom have I in heaven but Thee? and there is none upon earth that I desire beside Thee.' Marvellous testimony! But he only gets straight when he goes into the sanctuary and is quiet before God. Same here; in the sanctuary of God he beholds the power and glory of God.

You get into a terrible mess if you believe the idea that if you have sufficient faith and sufficient prayer, every illness, trouble and problem can be put right. The New Testament does not read like that. He does heal, He does cure, He does solve, He does prevent – but He allows others not to be healed, for His glory.

Think of the Bible itself. Paul is miraculously snatched away when a plot endangers his life; Stephen is stoned to death. Peter is delivered from prison; John the Baptist is beheaded. Jesus comes to his disciples in the storm on the lake and it is stopped; Paul is shipwrecked, though they're rescued. There are times when God miraculously delivers, and times when he doesn't. And you can only understand that if you submit it to the power and the glory of God. You can only rest back upon the glory of God in His purposes, which we do not fully understand, and won't until we meet Him.

If we understand the power and glory of God, then we know He *can* heal, and deliver and preserve us and so we pray for it. We don't give up praying for it, just as Paul prayed three times (in 2 Corinthians) for his own deliverance. And yet we also submit that prayer to the glory of God. The answer for Paul was that he was going to keep the thorn in the flesh; then he began to glory in his infirmities, because that's the way the power of God was going to rest on him. And that was going to glorify God; and *that* was his over-riding aim, not his deliverance from the thorn in the flesh. It's a hard thing to pray, and, so often, the purposes of God are much greater than we can understand.

And very often, some of the lovely things that God wants to do for us are subordinated to a bigger purpose. Zechariah and Elizabeth prayed for a child, but God delayed it until His moment in His purposes. Job had fixed ideas about sin and suffering; he argued with God. Suddenly God started questioning Job: 'Where were you when I laid the foundations of the earth? Then eventually, Job answered: 'I know that You can do all things.' That's the *power* of God. ' . . . And that no purpose of Yours can be thwarted.' That's the *glory* of God. And Job had to go through that experience until he could bow before the power and the glory of God.

Thirdly, here in verse 3 we have *the love of God*. Steadfast love; covenant love, or, if you have the Authorised Version, mercy. It comes right through the Old Testament. It's one of the most important words to learn. The steadfast love of the living God.

It's this love that the prophets got hold of again after the exile. All their hopes for the people of God seemed to be shattered, Jerusalem had fallen, the people of God had been taken away prisoners into exile. How could they explain this? How could God do this to His people? And though they cannot explain it there is one thing they lay hold of which does not alter, and it is the steadfast love of God. They work back to that. God's love is unchanging. For example, you get this in that most miserable of books, Lamentations. If you want a good weep, read Lamentations. If you feel miserably it really does beautifully for you. It's an absolutely miserable book, isn't it? Until suddenly you get to verse 23 and, like a rocket cascading into the darkness, comes that tremendous statement: 'The steadfast love of the Lord never ceases . . . great is Thy faithfulness.' The circumstances haven't altered. What's altered is that this man has got hold of the steadfast love of God. And isn't this what Romans 8 says to you and me as believers? 'Who shall separate us from the love of Christ?' You see, the New Testament does not say: 'You are a Christian, therefore you are going to avoid these things.' You are going to share with the rest of the world tribulation and distress. But none of them can separate you from the love of God.

The Bible does not say your circumstances are going to alter it. It says you are anchored by Christ through His Spirit into the love of God for ever. That is steadfast love. This is the love that saved us; the love that brought Jesus Christ into this world to die on the cross for your sake and mine. This is the love that hung upon the cross at Calvary. This is the love that brought us into His family, as we repented, and received, and believed.

Well, the Psalmist knew it, so at the very end of the psalm as he goes on he praises God; his soul is feasted. Verse 6: he meditates on his God (and does he not meditate on the centrality of God?). And he comes to verse 7, a verse I constantly use in hospital visiting. 'My soul,' he says to God, 'clings to You,' – and what happens? 'Your right hand upholds me.' As faith clings, so it proves. A marvellous verse! Write it on your bedroom mirror! Carry it with you. This is the anchor to the soul, of faith in the living God. 'O God, You are my God.' Christian, do you really believe in God?

SIN: THE BREAKING OF RELATIONSHIPS

by Rev. Chris Byworth

Let me start like this. Ask yourself an honest question: what really has, and usually does, upset you most in life?

My guess is that it isn't things like not having enough money or not getting on at work or failing exams or whatever it happens to be; it isn't those things that really upset you, it's when things are wrong between you and your husband/wife/children/boyfriend or girlfriend when relationships have broken down and are spoilt – I suspect that is what really upsets you. The essence of our life as God has made us is our relationships, and of course it's the essence of God's life. He is trinity, a threeness, in the love of the beloved and the love that binds them together. He is the perfect expression of relationship. That's why He is – why we call Him – Love. And God wants our lives to be lived out in a perfect set of relationships. We are all immeasurably enriched by each other, and the basic relationship of all is the relationship to God Himself.

Now, if the essence of life is relationships, the essence of sin is a breakdown in those relationships. The inevitable result of sin is the opposite of life, it's death – in all its horror and in all its meanings, the breakdown of our relationships here and in eternity. I believe God intends every human being to live in relationship four ways, and the last three flow from the first.

The first and basic one is *our relationship to God Himself*. God made us for Himself, to find joy and completion in a love-and-obedience relationship to Him. And that is what sin breaks first of all. The classic example of it is the Adam and Eve story. Even before they were sent out of the garden they sensed that they must hide, that something had broken, long before God underlined it and excluded them. The basic relationship that breaks is the one with God. And as a result the other three relationships from which our life is to be made up from break too.

The first of those three is *relationships with other people*. You see that again in the Adam and Eve story. The very first row brews up – 'The woman you gave me, she gave me the fruit and I ate.' Adam and Eve were meant to complement each other. That joyful joyous remark Adam made when he saw Eve – 'At last!' – the real thing! – 'at last *this* is bone of my bone' – within days, it has changed to 'the woman you gave me,' and the relationship has broken, it's spoilt. And the next story in the Bible is Cain and Abel. We see it in society today, it's basically exactly the same. We have created a society which is essentially competitive, in which it's each man and woman for himself, and we express surprise at the result; at the inadequacy, the destitution, the class hatred that is produced by that type of formula. The relationship with each other breaks.

And then there is that third relationship, *the relationship with the world of nature*. We were created to enjoy the natural world, but it is still profoundly true today that we still spoil the world we were made to have dominion over. We still cut down far too many trees and don't replace them, we still pollute the atmosphere, we still greedily use up the earth's limited resources, and so on.

There's one more relationship we don't often think of, but it's still there all right. *The relationship we have with our inner self.* It doesn't come out so obviously in the Adam and Eve story, but it's there just three chapters later. Genesis 6:5, 'And the Lord saw that every imagination of the thoughts of man's heart was only evil continually.' And a verse you may not know, a profound verse, Proverbs 8:36, 'He who sins against Me injures himself.' And we have the woeful tale today of mental illness and psychological instability and all the inner turmoil that is, indeed, in the hearts of many. The relationship within ourselves is wrecked as well. Those are the breakdowns in relationships; and the basic one is the relationship with God.

Now, what is at the heart of this breakdown? What is this 'sin' that causes this fourfold breakdown in relations? The way I want to look at it is to gather together the many words in the Bible for sin. I think there are something like sixteen in the Old Testament and another seven in the New. I don't think you could find a precise and different meaning for each one of them. But when you look at all of them together, one thing stands out immediately. The essence of sin is *something done against God.* It's marring God's image, failing to hit God's mark, not giving Him the honour due to Him. It's failing to meet His standards by not listening by mistake or – most terribly of all – by deliberate and repeated disobedience.

Now I find that obvious fact a very challenging one. I ask myself, and perhaps I dare ask you too, why is it that I don't mind admitting my sins to God – not even my most inmost and personal ones; and yet I am exceedingly uptight if other Christians realise that I am anything less than perfect, and I'm very defensive about letting on and *very* quick to defend myself if someone else criticises? Is it because I am concerned about my image as a leader? Ought I not to be far more concerned that God and my relationship with Him is being spoilt? King David grossly oversimplified when, after murdering Uriah and committing adultery with Bathsheba, he cried out 'Against Thee, against Thee only, have I sinned' – he hadn't only, had he? – but he had got to the nub of the problem. Sin is essentially against God.

From all the many Hebrew and Greek words I think there are two basic notions that emerge, and they are summed up in the Church of England's 'General Confession': 'We have left undone those things that we ought to have done' – element one – 'and we have done those things we ought not to have done' – element two. I'm going to look at sin under those two headings.

1. Sin is what we have left undone that we should have done

We need to be clear about this. The idea of falling short, of not doing every time what we should and not giving God what is His by right is basic to most of the words that deal with sin. The main Greek word is *Hamartia*, which comes forty-eight times in the Letter to the Romans, and if you look at Romans 3:23 you've got it there – 'All have sinned and come short of the glory of God.' Paul is saying that we are far less than the glory of God that we were made to reflect. We are a constant disappointment.

But there is a more precise and telling kind of falling short, and it comes out in two other more precise words, *Adikia* and *Asebeia*, two Greek words that stress our failure to give God the love, obedience and reverence which it is His due to receive and our privilege to give. It is this which is the basic sin of omission – ourselves at the centre of our lives, and God remaining on the fringe. We may call Him in at crises or on Sundays, for a quiet time or to deal with a particular sin that is as it were 'on our list' – smoking, drinking, whatever your particular sin is. But *we* remain at the centre. I ask myself and I ask you, how far have we even begun to ask ourselves what God feels about the complex social, political and economic issues of our day – and, nearer home, the whole presuppositions on which we run our family lives, or the very basis of what is going on in our work which we do for forty hours a week? There are whole areas of our lives where we are in the centre, and God, if He is there at all, is on the circumference. I believe that for many Christians, God is only at the centre of small portions of their lives – those portions with easy answers and traditional guidance which is not too painful. 'We have left undone those things which we ought to have done.'

2. Sin is secondly the doing of those things which we ought not to have done

Again, there is a whole range of words to express the different facets of what disobedience is. There's a word which means 'to slip up because you are not concentrating'. You say things you don't really mean and then you realise the consequences. I think the reason is very often simply that you are not close enough to God. But there's a more serious word which means 'choosing not to hear'. Like children when you tell them to tidy the garden or do their homework. But we're like that too; we don't respond when God tells us to do something. We don't have quiet times, we don't read a book or go to a meeting because we are afraid that God may indeed speak to us. I know that's happened in my experience. You need to be sure as a Christian that you're doing the right thing. You need to think it through, you need to listen to God if He is telling you to think it through. But the most serious word – and the most frequent word – for 'not doing what you ought to have done' is a word that means we know perfectly well what God wants us to do, think or say – and we refuse repeatedly and deliberately to do it. There is a Hebrew word and a Greek word with this basic idea – sin is knowing God's law and deliberately breaking it. As Paul points out in Romans 2, those who know God's laws (as we presumably do) will be held most responsible if they break them. The Adam and Eve story is precisely that – the story of disobedience. We as their successors inherit that same tendency to be dissatisfied with their tremendous and wonderful responsibility and to grasp for more. It takes a second Adam to reverse the process by doing exactly the opposite; by not grasping on to what was His by right, His glory, and by spending His life in total disobedience to His heavenly Father. An obedience that led finally and decisively to the cross.

So, sin is breaking God's law knowingly and deliberately, sin is standing up for one's rights, ensuring that we dominate a particular relationship, ensuring that at least *we* are not put out – which is the opposite of the way of Jesus. 'I don't see why I should apologise – it's not my fault – well, hardly at all, I'm going to wait for them to make the first move.' 'I have to go along with their whole approach in my job, you simply can't get involved in this business without doing things that way.' 'It's more than my job's worth.' I don't see why I should break off this friendship with so-and-so, I might be able to influence them for Christ.' And so on. Sin is doing what we ought not to do.

I think one of the most tragic sights we see is when you see children with their parents openly ignoring them, blatantly flouting them or being rude. Of course there are often genuine reasons why this happens – possibly it is part of growing up (not that it makes it right) – but if you think of us as the children and God the Father who not only made us but bought us back at that appalling price; and then think that we are like that, ignoring Him and flouting Him and even resenting Him; and if you realise that this is what sin is, saying and doing and thinking what we know is wrong – then you begin to realise that sin is a very horrid thing.

I want to summarise now. Life is about relationships and especially about our relationship with God. Sin is about the spoiling of those relationships which results from the spoiling of our relationship with God. Sin in both its aspects is a very horrid thing, and of course it puts us under the power of Satan, and all our relationships become increasingly, progressively, disintegrated. We grow bigger and bigger in the centre of things; we become our world. We become incapable of giving and receiving love. We have marred the image of God the Father who made us, wounded the love of God the Son who died for us, and quenched the fire, life and joy of God the Holy Spirit who longs to indwell us. Only when we truly realise the wonder of Christ will we truly hate and turn from that which is wrong and that which we know is wrecking us and our world.

We need to echo the horror of Paul: 'Wretched man that I am! Who will deliver me from this body of death?' We need also to echo his praise: 'Thanks be to God through our Lord Jesus Christ.'

465 ✓
much

FAILING TO SPEAK TO MEN

by Rev. George Duncan

2 Kings 7:9

✓ The theme that's been laid on my heart is this: failing to speak to men. I want to consider what I call the sin of silence, because I believe that if there's any sin of which the Christian church is more guilty than any other, it's this. You know, the Bible tells us that sins of omission are no less sins. 'To him that knoweth to do good and doeth it not, to him it is sin.' I believe the worst sinners are not those who do what's wrong, but the ones who don't do what's right. It's worth thinking that through.

I want to base our study on some words from the seventh chapter of the second book of Kings. It's a long passage, and I'm going to assume you'll be seeing our text in its context as we go along. It's a statement from verse 9, and I shall be reading from the Authorised Version.

✓ Then they said one to another [these four leprous men, who had discovered the deserted camp of the Syrians, and were enjoying all they found there]: We do not well: this day is a day of good tidings, and we hold our peace.

The sin of silence. The four leprous men passed through changing moods and emotions; for them it was a day of good tidings. And so surely it is still for us, for that is how our gospel has been described – 'Good News'.

The situation historically was quite simple: Samaria was besieged by the invading hosts of Syria. The city was in a desperate plight. Cannibalism was rife as the people starved. The four lepers were trapped between the enemy and the city walls. The city was closed to them: to approach the enemy meant immediate death. Then, suddenly, all was changed, because God had stepped into the situation. Let's look at these four men.

First of all I want to note with you that *these men were amazed at what they found.* Verses 3 to 7 tell of their experience. It was a desperate situation. There was no possible escape. They were hopeless and helpless. I believe we too are living in days when an increasing sense of hopelessness and helplessness is gripping the minds of all thinking people.

We see the misery in which these four men were placed, but we see the mystery with which they were faced, for in their desperation they arose to go to the camp of the Syrians, and, we read, 'When they were come to the uttermost part of the camp of Syria, behold, there was no man there.' The Lord had intervened; the forces that threatened to destroy had been scattered, and into the darkness of their despair light suddenly had shined with a brilliance that both dazed and dazzled them. God had stepped in.

So it is with men today. The whole message of the Christian faith concerns the intervention of God in human life. God acted in Christ, and through that intervention and through what God has done and will do, we believe in a Christ who did come, who still comes, and who will come. A God who intervenes and who will save. Surely, surely we are amazed at what we have found.

Secondly, *these men were absorbed with what they had got.* Everything was theirs for the taking. Those who before had nothing, had everything. Did they need food?

It was there in abundance. Drink? They could take their fill and quench their thirst. Dress? They could replace their rags. Wealth? They could fill their pockets and take sackfuls of silver and gold besides. They had been paupers; now they were princes. And so too is it with the Christian. In complete contradiction to the popular misconception that the Christian life is impoverished, it is incredibly enriched. Paul speaks of the unsearchable riches of Christ. God so loved that He gave. He still loves, He still gives. Every single need of the human heart is offered freely to us in Christ. In Him we are multi-millionaires!

In verse 8 we see those men having a wonderful time. If anyone had asked them how they were getting on, they would have said, 'We are having a great time, and it's wonderful to be here.' It would have been true. It's true of the Christian experience too; it's meant to be that way. The Bible tells us of a God who gives us all things richly to enjoy. I get disturbed at the way so many preach the word and the gospel in tones of funereal gloom – as if it were the worst of news instead of the best.

It was meant to be that way; God is our Father, he loves us. Every father wants his children to experience real joy and God is no different. It was meant to be that way – but not to *stay* that way.

So the four men went the final step. They were amazed at what they had found; they were absorbed with what they had got – and *they were ashamed of what they had done*. 'We do not well: this day is a day of good tidings, and we hold our peace.'

The sin of silence. When did you last speak to anybody about Christ? When did you last invite anybody to your church? When? I want to note the sin that troubled these men. '*We hold our peace.*' They were leaving the thousands in the doomed city uninformed, dying in their misery. We talk today about the silent majority. Possibly the most grievous sin in the church of Christ today is that we are in the silent majority. How many lives are we in touch with, with whom we have earned the right to speak? I am not talking of speaking roughly or rudely or discourteously, sometimes going up to people and asking if they are saved. I'm thinking of the people we are in touch with, with whom we have from time to time the right, the responsibility and the opportunity to say something – and we say nothing. I wonder how God evaluates our respectable silence?

A sin that troubled them – and a sight that thrilled them. What was that sight? Surely that of the people flocking out of the city and finding their every need met. To begin with the message was met with incredulity, suspicion; but finally they were convinced and they came out in their thousands. Every now and then the Christian may be privileged to see such sights. I don't think any of us who shared in the first crusade by Billy Graham at Harringay will ever forget those tremendous evenings. But it's only from time to time that we are privileged to see that kind of thing. Some people criticise big crusades. I know they have their dangers, but I think some people would have criticised the Day of Pentecost – too many people, a bit of emotionalism – forgetting that the Holy Spirit individualises in the crowd. But oh, how one longs to see revival coming to our privileged land, where things are so stodgy! Going around the world and seeing what God is doing in other countries makes you think. The thing that's fascinating to me is that it is not happening because of great preaching, although biblical preaching lies at the heart of it; it's not even happening because of great Billy Graham crusades, although Billy is having his crusades and I'll say, 'God bless Billy'; it's happening because ordinary Christians are sharing their faith. That's all. People, finding such satisfaction, such a total answer in Jesus Christ that they are sharing it with their friends; using – not a trap, necessarily but maybe a teapot (or, in America, a coffee pot).

Have you ever used your teapot for Christ? Turned your fireside chair into your pulpit? With your congregation of one, sitting in the solitary pew on the other side of the fireplace, and the opportunity, not forcing things, but because you've prayed a lot for that soul and cared a lot for them, of swinging the conversation round to the church or the minister or vicar, or the Master Himself? Have you ever done that kind of thing? Or are we just a great congregation of sinners, guilty of the sin of silence?

The sight that thrilled them was only possible when the silence was broken. What need there is for faith to become vocal, whether it's in the Press, on television, on the shop floor, in the board room or the staff room; the sin of silence has got the church in its grip.

How many people have you told? Jesus told us to tell the world, and the world begins at your doorstep and mine. A Christian lady coming out of a supermarket was sensitive and observant. There was no queue, no line at the cash desk as the girl totted up the figures. When she had paid her bill and got her change, the Christian lady looked at the girl and said, 'Is everything all right?' The girl broke down and wept. It wasn't all right. But nobody had cared.

God cares, desperately. The Bible says, and I believe it, 'God does not will that any should perish, but that all should be saved.' To make it possible, Christ gave His life a ransom for all. God has given you your personality, all your resources available to you in the Holy Spirit, all the contacts that He wants you to have. He wants you to live in Christ, but He wants you to speak. 'You shall receive power,' said Jesus, 'after the Holy Ghost is come upon you, and you shall be witnesses unto Me.' A witness talks. When did you last talk about Jesus when you had earned the right and God had given you the opportunity? Not rudely, but caringly? Not doing all the talking, but ready to listen and then showing the remedy, that you have found a Saviour who died for us and wants to dwell in us with all his fullness.

The sin of silence. In my judgement it's the most grievous sin in the Christian church here at home today. Are you guilty of it? Am I?

'We do not well: this day is a day of good tidings, and we hold our peace.'

THE SECOND TIME

by Rev. Eric Alexander

Jonah 3:1

If I were to say the word 'Jonah', I can guarantee that for nearly all of us the word that would come into our minds would be 'whale'. But the fact is that the 'great fish' of 1:17 occupies a very secondary place in the message of the book of Jonah.

The real issue is a most remarkable and widespread work of the grace of God issuing in repentance and a return to God which took place in the city of Nineveh and – as we read in 3:5 – reached from the highest to the lowest in the land. The people believed God, proclaimed a fast, put on sackcloth from the greatest to the least of them, and there was a mighty outpouring of the Spirit of God in Nineveh.

The striking thing is that you don't get to that theme until the third of four chapters. The first two chapters, and indeed the last one, are taken up not with God's dealings with Nineveh but with Jonah, His poor disobedient and unhappy servant.

It's a missionary story, of course, and Jonah is often described as the reluctant missionary. But I want to focus, not on Jonah's reluctance, but that of God. The reluctance of God to leave this child of His in the miseries of disobedience, to cease being gracious to this fractious, rebellious and unhappy servant. So our text is 3:1: 'Then the word of the Lord came to Jonah the second time.'

Some time ago, I was talking to a young Christian worker who had been utterly disabled spiritually by the devil. On one occasion in his life he had stepped out of God's will in conscious, quite deliberate disobedience. And he said to me, 'I am condemned to live for the rest of my days in God's second best.' Now I want to ask: does Scripture give warrant to believe that of God, and His dealings with His children? That when a man turns a deaf ear to God, he is condemned to live in God's second best? I want to say to you from Jonah that God is the God of the second word, of the second chance and of the second time. 'The word of the Lord came to Jonah the second time . . . ' – and the God who thus met with Jonah has given a major place in His providence to the grace of repentance and mercy towards His unhappy children.

I want to look with you at the message of this part of Jonah and concentrate on three things. Firstly, *upon Jonah as the man who needed this second word from God.*

I suppose the most significant thing about Jonah is that he was a servant and prophet of God. But the really frightening thing is that Jonah had reached the point where the work that God had called him to, and his plans for that work, had become more important than God. I deduce that about Jonah because he was determined to serve God in a place where God had not sent him and to live his life without reference to God. And he was neither the first nor the last man to do it. He had turned his back on the word of God for himself.

Now that's a grave danger for a man who is a servant of God. And (if I may address my brother ministers, and I say it deeply to my own soul) one of the gravest dangers of our ministry of the word of God is that we imagine so easily that we have discharged our duty to the word of God by preaching on it. 'Oh! That's a great truth and it can fire our soul! What shall I do with it? I'll preach on it!' Thereby we can be deflecting the word of God in all its fullness, from our own lives. And I would imagine that Jonah had preached about the very things he was being disobedient about himself. It was as clear as a bell: 'The word of the Lord came to Jonah the son of Amittai, saying, Arise, go to Nineveh . . . ' Like many of us, Jonah's problem wasn't with the bits that he couldn't understand, but with the bit of God's word that he *could*. God said to Jonah 'This is where I want you to go.' And Jonah – not, I think, with noise or commotion but secretly, in his heart – said 'I have different plans for my life. I have a better way, in my judgement, to be your servant.' And from that point there was a controversy raging between God and Jonah. I am not sure that Jonah was aware of the depth of it. 1:5, they went into the ship and found that Jonah was fast asleep. The storm that raged about that ship was the outward sign of the controversy raging between God and Jonah; and at this point Jonah appears as a man whose life belies his testimony. He was urged to the point (1:9) where he had to speak: 'I am a Hebrew and I fear the Lord the God of heaven who made the sea and the dry land.' A fine, biblical testimony to God the Creator. The only trouble was, it wasn't true; the universal result in Scripture of fearing God is obeying Him. But the only person Jonah was interested in pleasing was himself. The heathen in the ship just couldn't make him out. They were saying: if you desire to please God, why are you running away from Him? There was a great credibility gap in his life and his testimony. This happens when a man is in secret flight from God. You don't need to get up and take a ship anywhere for this to be true in the deep places of your life.

Now the amazing thing is that in this condition where Jonah's life belied his testimony, Jonah's message to these sailors seems to have born fruit in their lives. Do you notice in 1:14, they become praying men ('We beseech

Thee') who feared the Lord ('O Lord, let us not perish . . . '). They feared Jonah's God exceedingly. They offered a sacrifice, they made vows; they had some sort of commitment to God, and, clearly, it all happened because of Jonah's testimony. There lies a solemn warning that usefulness in God's service is never a guarantee of the condition of a man's heart.

So he began to experience the deep unhappiness of a man in controversy with God (2:2, 4:2). He knew what it was not only to be in utter isolation but also to feel that God had cast him off. It's one of the appalling miseries of this kind of situation. It is at this point that the focus of Jonah's praying changes. In 2:7 he cries out 'When my soul fainted within me I remembered the Lord.' That was where hope dawned for Jonah.

There comes a time when you have to stop thinking about yourself and your sin, and Jonah had come to that point. In the Psalms you so often find men of God who have got to these depths and suddenly they find God raising their head to look away from themselves and their sin; and they say like the Psalmist in Psalm 42, 'Why art thou cast down, O my soul? . . . I shall yet praise Him for the help of His countenance.'

That brings us to our second point: *the God who restored Jonah.* Let me point out to you some of the things Jonah discovered about God in his disobedience.

More than anything else, he discovered that God's grief over our failure is exceeded only by His grace after it. Have you grasped that truth? Jonah had exhausted himself. He had exhausted the resources of all kinds of people and situations, but one thing he had not exhausted was the grace of God.

In whatever sense you know yourself to be utterly exhausted at this moment, there is one thing you will never exhaust, and that is the grace of God in all its tenderness and sweetness and personal care for you which makes the very heart of God open toward you. And for Jonah every move that God made in his life and circumstances was a new evidence of that grace. The storm was a storm of grace; God was in it; the fish was the provision of grace, and God sent it. The recommissioning of Jonah was a word of grace, and God spoke it.

The devil has a two-pronged attack here. Firstly he comes and entices you into disobedience, making light of it. Doubtless this was what happened with Jonah. Why *should* you go? What possible harm *could* there be in staying where you are? Look at the need in *this* place . . . Or he'll say: 'What harm is there in doing that? You can still carry on as before, afterwards.' He said it to Adam and Eve in Eden: 'You will be like gods.' But then when you have fallen he turns his other face and you sit in the ruins of your sin, and he says, 'Well, you've really done it now, haven't you? There's no way back out of that mess.' Have you ever known that, my Christian friend? Have you known what it is to have the pressure of the evil one holding you down?

When he comes like that you need to answer with Jonah, 'When my soul fainted within me I remembered the Lord.' That opened up a whole new vista for Jonah; and the climax of it was when he came to that place when, out of the fish and landed on dry ground, the word of the Lord came to him the second time. I scarcely think Jonah was surprised, for the glory of God's grace had dawned upon him afresh. We need to learn to say what Jonah was really saying out of the depth of that great darkness: 'Rejoice not against me, O my adversary; when I fall I shall rise again . . . deliverance belongs to the Lord.' And the fish vomited him out, saying: the Lord has done everything He meant to do in you, Jonah, you can go on to dry land now.

And Jonah found that this grace was designed not only to raise him out of the darkness and misery of his failures and restore him to the presence and favour of God. It was a grace that was ready to recommission him for the very ministry where his failure had occurred. Isn't that astonishing? On all common sense grounds you would never have sent Jonah back to Nineveh, would you? But, you see, God has restoration for His servant, restoring him for a destiny of blessing and significance in God's service.

The other main thing Jonah learned about God was that His power is as boundless as His grace. He was not a helpless spectator, He was in the midst of the situation.

God moves in a mysterious way
His wonders to perform
He plants His footsteps in the sea
And rides upon the storm.

Now finally, what about *the way Jonah was restored and given the second chance.* 'The word of the Lord came to Jonah the second time . . . ' Really, God's normal way of acting is by His word. It may be that what some of us need to do is to allow God just to speak His word to us. Jonah was restored when the word of the Lord came to him and he repented and obeyed Him. Now, what was that repentance? Well, it was really a dying to self and a rising to newness of life. The way back for Jonah was the way of death, burial and resurrection from the waves of the sea, and there is a very real way in which he provides not only a sign of the death and resurrection of Jesus, but a pattern of the way by which God brings us back.

It may be infinitely costly to come back to God. It was for Jonah. The anguish of the second chapter is profound and beyond our understanding. But you remember what Jesus said? 'Except a corn of wheat fall into the ground and die it abides alone, but if it die it brings forth much fruit.' And Jonah had to learn what it was to die to selfish ambition, to die to his own plans and purpose, to die to everything that centred upon Jonah; and he was raised up out of the entangling weeds to the place where he cried out, 'I will pay that that I have vowed.'

Well, my Christian brother or sister, where are you at this moment? Somehow in God's second best? Well, I want to say to you that God comes to you with a second word. A word of restoration. You can never drift out of God's hands. Let me put it another way, in the picture that was given to another prophet. As Jeremiah watched the potter at work, God said to him, 'Can I not do with you as this potter?'

He is saying to you, 'Cannot I do with you, can I not mould and restore you?' And there is only one answer. It is 'Lord, you can! For your mercy's sake do it, and start it now.'

THE FINISHED WORK OF CHRIST

by Rev. J. Alec Motyer

Colossians 3:1–4

I want to share with you some thoughts on 'the finished work of Christ', so that we may learn together what it is that He has finished, and then ask ourselves the question, what have we got to do about it? How do we respond to this truth?

Now the simplest reality in connection with the finished work of Christ touches the Lord Jesus Himself. He went to the cross once for all; and, having suffered, He will never have to suffer again. That is a glorious and a moving thing when we ponder (as far as Scripture permits us) the reality of the Lord Jesus Christ's sufferings. What he did He did once for all, and dying, as far as the Lord Jesus is concerned, is over and done with. It is a thing of the past – it is part of the finished work of Christ.

But another and vital part of the work is this, that He has nothing more to do as far as His Father is concerned. I want to speak reverently as well as plainly, so may I put it this way. The Lord Jesus could die on the cross a thousand times, yet no salvation would be accomplished until God in heaven was satisfied with what His Son had done. If the work of Christ is to be finished it is essential that it be finished in the estimation of God. It is to this that the Lord Jesus referred speaking to the disciples (in

John 16) when he says that the Holy Spirit, making His voice heard, will convince the world of the righteousness of the Lord Jesus 'because I go to the Father, and you see me no more'. He is going to the Father to report back to the One who sent Him; He is going to say before the throne, 'Mission accomplished!' And if He is welcome, if He is retained with His Father 'so that you see me no more' – then we will indeed know that Jesus is righteous as far as His Father is concerned.

Don't you think that the Father's heart longed to snatch His Son there and then from the cross to the throne? There is a wonderful deliberation about the acts of God that followed the crucifixion of our Lord Jesus. Grasp it: the works of God are deliberate so that we may learn the mind of God. It as though the Father pondered for three days the claim registered by Jesus on the cross, 'It is finished!'

'Is it truly finished?' the Father might be pictured asking Himself. 'Did He do all that I sent Him to do? Did He teach all that I sent Him to teach? Was He perfect in his character and life as I meant Him to be perfect, and – above all – did He really save the sinners I sent Him to save?' And on the third day the Father raised Him from the dead, so that we might know the estimate the Father placed on the Son. And on the fortieth day the Father raised Him with equal deliberation from the face of this earth until a cloud received Him and Jesus took his place at the Father's right hand in the heavenly places – so that we might know the estimate that the Father places on the Son. Therefore, how right the hymn:

> Because the sinless Saviour died, my soul is counted free
> For God is satisfied.

Finished as far as He is concerned; finished as far as the Father is concerned. Now, the third dimension of the finished work of Christ – finished as far as *we* are concerned. There is nothing more that He has to do for us; all His work is ended! Let's see this in Colossians chapters 2 and 3. Four affirmations are made about the Christian. One, in 2:20, *If you died with Christ* (it is an affirmation, there is no doubt attached); two, in 3:1, *You were raised with Christ*; three, in 3:3, *Your life is hid with Christ in God,* and four, in 3:4, *Then shall you also appear with Him in glory.* So the passage takes us through these four cardinal truths about Jesus: His *death,* His *resurrection,* His *ascension,* and His *second coming;* and it says that in each the Christian believer is identified with Christ.

What does this mean? What is the Scripture saying when it says, when He died, we died? When He rose, we rose? When He ascended, we ascended, and when He comes again we come with Him? Well, it's saying this. It's saying first of all that according to God's will and deed the fully paid penalty of sin has been credited to our account. When Jesus died *we died;* the full reality and meaning of His death has been credited to us. Then, the full reality of a new life has been credited to us. Notice the past tense – you *were* raised. It's not something that was credited to the believer the moment that Jesus rose.

And thirdly, your life is hid with Christ in God. The Bible insists on the factuality of our Lord's resurrection. You will find, in the glorious account of it in the first chapter of Acts, that the visibility of it is stated five times over. It is as if the Holy Spirit is saying 'I don't want you to be uncertain about this; it really happened.' Your life is hid with Christ in God. The Father has granted to us, here and now, the eternal security of a life already established in heaven. I will share the heavenly place; His servants will serve Him and see His face – but that will not *add* to our security, for at this moment – as those who have been identified with Jesus – our life is hid with Christ in God.

And fourthly, the consummation of it all will be this. 'Then shall you also appear with Him in glory.' A sure hope. When the Lord Jesus appears in the glory of His second coming, His saints will be manifested in their true colours at His side. But consider: when the Lord Jesus comes, He will not don any *new* glory for the occasion. 'This same Jesus' (Acts 1) – you watched Him go, but He will come trailing clouds of glory; He will be manifested as the glorious Christ. But no different! He will show then the glory that He possesses now.

Likewise (may God write this on our minds with clear understanding) – when the believer is at that day manifested with Christ it will be in the glory that is true of him now, that was purchased for him on Calvary; the glory of the ascended life: the glory which is our true reality *at this moment*. And that is part of the meaning of this great phrase, 'the finished work of Christ'. He wrought everything that He intends to work for your behalf and mine.

Now I want to ask you, did you know that? It is not an experience we are to seek, it is a truth that we are to accept. It is couched in past tenses. It is something that is *already* affirmatively true of the Christian believer. Did you know that? Will you bow your head to the truth? Say, 'Yes Lord, I accept, on the authority of Your word, that that is the real truth. You, my Father, have accredited to me the finished work of Christ.'

There is so much in me that this point wants to rise up and say, 'Wouldn't it be nice?' Do you find yourself like that? 'I don't *feel* better, I don't *feel* as if the finished work of Christ has been accredited to my account and made real in me. I don't find it like that, I find that day by day I am subject to sin as though my life had not been dealt with on the cross. I find myself acting out the old life and not the new life – as though I had never been raised with Christ.'

But when you come before the word of God you come before the specialist's diagnosis. Many a doctor stands by many a bedside and says to many a patient, 'You're cured; there is no longer any trace of your disease.' And the patient says, 'I neither feel that nor find it. I do not feel myself to be cured. I know that if I were to rise out of my bed now I would collapse with weakness.' 'Nevertheless,' says the specialist, 'you are cured.' And in the deepest reality of God, the Father *has* accredited to us the finished work of Christ. I don't ask you therefore to feel it. I don't ask you, 'Do you find it?' But I do ask you, 'Do you believe it?' For that is the reality about every Christian. That is what the specialist says. That is the Christian's true identity – a man or woman, identified with the Lord Jesus.

We have to learn from the Bible not only what the truth is, but also how we are to respond to the truth. What an important statement that is! May I briefly sketch for you, for your further study, how this passage not only tells us what is truth but also tells us what to do.

Seek the things which are above. (Chapter 3:1). Since you were raised with Christ, this is what you are to do. Verse 2, set your mind on the things which are above. If we are to grow in the experience of what God has made true of us, then we must look to our aims. What are we seeking in life? Then we must look to our minds, what we are thinking about. Our aims, and our minds, and between them our vision. Seek the things that are above, where Christ is seated at the right hand of God. The clarity of our vision of the Lord Jesus in his His own person and His ascended royal dignity.

If we are to grow in the feeling and the finding of this thing that is true of us, what are our aims? What are our thoughts? And is the Lord Jesus constantly clear in our vision?

LIFT UP YOUR EYES

by Rev. Andrew Dow

Psalm 121

Sometimes in the course of parish visiting I ask people if they would like me to read a favourite passage of Scripture to them, and the most frequently asked for is Psalm 23. But perhaps second in the popularity charts is Psalm 121, and it's this lovely Psalm I want to look at now. In many ways, of course, the message is similar to Psalm 23. Both speak of the protection of God; both have a wide, an eternal, perspective with the last verse in each case reaching out to the furthest imaginable point in the future. So Psalm 121:8, 'The Lord will keep your going out and your coming in from this time forth and for evermore.'

Now it is that word *keep* which is the theme word of this psalm. It comes six times in eight verses. Verse 5 puts it most simply, but it appears also in verses 3, 4, and (twice) in verse 7. Keep, keep, keep – that's the refrain; what one commentator has described as the Psalmist's amulet against all fears and phobias. Notice the emphasis; on the keeper, not on the dangers. It's an interesting emphasis.

As with many of the Psalms, in order to 'get the meat off the bone' we've got to examine the background. You'll observe that in some versions this psalm has a heading: 'Song of Ascents'. If that note is authentic it gives us a clue. Here is a Jewish pilgrim going up to Jerusalem. He is, quite literally, ascending. Jerusalem is some 2,300 feet up, and so for the Jew coming from the Mediterranean coast in the west, or the southern desert, or from Galilee in the north, there was a climb on to the hills of southern Judea. Almost certainly these are the hills in verse 1. 'I lift up my eyes to the hills.' That was a good thing to do. You and I constantly need the reminder to look up, because when left to ourselves we're all too inclined to look down. So the Bible says many times over, 'Look up, Christian, look up!'

And so the Psalmist did, and he took his eyes off the blazing dusty road at his feet whence naturally his gaze had fallen; and he looked up, and there were those hills around Jerusalem, beautiful, inspiring and refreshing. Yes, a good thing to do – a step in the right direction.

But curiously enough it wasn't the whole answer to his need. Because immediately a question arises in his mind. Verse 1 (second half): 'Whence does my help come from?'

Some versions don't make this a question, but that's misleading. The question mark is right. 'I see the hills, Lord, but where does my help *really* come from?' And the answer is in verse 2: 'My help comes from the Lord, who made the heaven and the earth.' The hills are a symbol of great strength, but the strength that I need is not really there. It lies in the Lord who made those hills. Better to look at hills than a dusty road, but my gaze must go further and deeper, to God Himself.

And you and I are on our pilgrimage, and we can lift our eyes and see many hills of help which God has put round us. Our church, the local fellowship, our friends, our family, our Christian experience, our training, our teaching – tremendously helpful, but, good as they all are, they are not infallible. We must look further, to the Lord behind them. I've noticed some people say to me 'I do love my church, I couldn't do without my church.'

And – while it's a pleasant change to hear appreciation of the establishment – such a remark always raises a little question mark in my mind: 'Does this good soul know the Lord of the church, the maker of the hills?' Because it's that that matters. If all outward fellowship were to disappear (as well it might one day in this country) would there still be a meaningful spiritual life without it – a relationship with God Himself? May I ask you this; is your trust in the Lord, or in the hills?

And so to verse 3, 'He will not let your foot be moved.' Do you notice a change? There's a change of focus now. The 'I' and 'my' of verses 1 and 2 have become 'your' and so it remains through to verse 8. It may well be that this psalm was later used in corporate worship, sung by successive journeys of pilgrims journeying to Jerusalem. Verses 1 and 2 would be intoned by a lead singer, solo, to be answered by a rousing chorus of those behind him. What an effective way that must have been of presenting the truth! What an encouragement as they marched on, a hymn of mutual support.

In verses 3 to 6 we can see the situation of the pilgrims beautifully mirrored, on the move and in their nightly encampments; verse 3, they're on the march – 'He will not let your foot be moved.' No stumbling in the way. And then they're at rest – 'He who keeps you will not slumber.' In those days, when you travelled in the Holy Land you hired yourself a keeper to watch over you while you slept. The trouble was that those hired keepers would sometimes fall asleep themselves. Not so the Lord Himself. 'He will neither slumber nor sleep.' Totally reliable!

Then verse 5, on the move again. 'The Lord is your keeper . . . the sun shall not smite you by day, nor the moon by night.' Why that? Well, of course the moon gave necessary illumination to burglars and bandits, who would be a constant threat to all travellers; what Psalm 91:5 calls 'the terror of the night'. From these the Lord will give protection. But there's a deeper meaning. Sunstroke was a real peril, but what about moonstroke? It doesn't exist, you say. No, but people thought it did. Whence the word lunatic? And the Orientals used to believe that the moon shed malignant influences on unsuspecting sleepers. What we've got here is, you see, perils real and imagined; and the Lord protects from both.

We've all got fears for the future, some reasonable, some groundless yet strong; the Lord is our keeper from them all. That unknown area from which, we have a sort of lurking fear, some ill-defined attack is going to come – that's under the Lord's control! Perhaps in your case it's something physical, fear of illness maybe; or some illness or problem of the mind which has troubled you in the past and every now and then it's as if it's going to come back again. 'The sun shall not smite you by day, nor the moon by night.'

Perils real, perils imagined; God's cover is fully comprehensive. Verse 7: 'The Lord will keep you from all evil; He will keep your life.' The Psalmist's trust in the Lord widens and deepens as he warms to his theme. 'The Lord will keep you from all evil.' And yet doesn't this raise a problem if you're thinking carefully about the meaning of these words, as we view this claim in the light of the facts of everyday life? Does the Lord really protect His servants from all evil? Then what about the Christian family whose house is ransacked while they're away? It happens. Or the car accident that causes serious hurt to the Christian leader? It happens. Or the child of the Christian family who gets into wrong company and into serious trouble with the authorities? It happens. If we're being really honest with ourselves, one could be forgiven for thinking that the Pilgrim Psalmist has let his enthusiasm run away with him in verse 7: life just isn't like that.

We could, but I hope that instead we'll seek the truth

by thinking more deeply. Maybe by setting one Scripture alongside another and so arriving at the full counsel of God. Clearly, the Christian has no divine immunity from hurt or trouble. You've only got to read about the sufferings of Paul to understand that. How then do we read verse 7? It promises that all evil will be averted from him who has the Lord for his keeper. So – if any so-called evil comes, the Christian can be sure it's good 'with a veil on'; he may regard it as such and work it out as such. That's what Paul meant in his famous promise, 'We know that in everything God is working for good with those who love Him.' Even when the Christian cannot see the why or wherefore, he knows that there is God's love in and behind His workings, and deep down he can keep calm.

In the light of that, may we dare to paraphrase verse 7 just slightly? 'The Lord will keep you from the ultimate corruption of evil.' From the devil, if you like. Whatever is thrown at us, God's servant will not sink without trace because he's kept busy by the Master Keeper – and that interpretation is supported by the second half of verse 7, 'He will keep your life.' Our soul or personal being – the deepest part of us.

One commentator put it this way: 'Whatever may be shorn away by the sharp shears of loss, your soul will be safe; and if it is, nothing else matters.' Nothing else matters . . . Jesus put it like this, didn't He? Don't worry about those who have power to destroy the body. In other words, those who can inflict lots of apparent evil. Rather, fear the soul-keeper Himself. If you belong to Him this afternoon, He'll keep your soul – it's absolutely safe in this life and the next. That's a great assurance!

We've noted already how in verse 8 the perspective stretches out to eternity. As he draws to a close, the Psalmist returns to his favourite antithesis of day and night, work and rest. 'The Lord will keep your going out and your coming in.' A lovely way of describing the daily cycle of external toil, and repose in the home – the two halves of the pilgrim life for every Christian; for you and me, going out and coming in. And in both – in all – the Lord promises to keep us.

Lift up your eyes, therefore, lift up your eyes to the hills. Yes, but further than that; to the Lord who made the hills. And rest secure in Him.

LORD OF THE CRISIS

by Rev. Andrew MacRae

Mark 9:14–27

I wanted to read this story with you, because it is descriptive of Jesus as *Lord of the crisis.*

I've no doubt that every Christian believer is as convinced as I am that Jesus Christ is Lord. We recognise that this is the essence of the faith; didn't Paul say, 'If thou shalt confess with thy mouth Jesus as Lord and that God hath raised Him from the dead, thou shalt be saved'? For us, for believing Christian men, women and young people, Christ is Lord. Lord of life and death, Lord of the church and all creation, Lord of history and the cosmos. Lord of all. Yet, far too many of us cherish that concept of the Lord Jesus Christ as an idea in the mind, rather than as an influence in the life.

We were reminded in the first of Eric Alexander's Bible Readings* that God intends to renew our minds, that we are to think our way through to the will of God. That's what we were told from Scripture – 'that ye may prove what is that good, and acceptable, and perfect, will of God.' Similarly, if we *have* thought our way through to the lordship of Christ, it should also be in order to put that lordship into practice in our daily lives. And nowhere is that more important than when you are in

*To be found on p.53 of this book.

one of life's crises. There's no point, you see, in professing the lordship of Christ – unless you practise it.

You are all familiar with Peter's great contradiction in Acts chapter 11: 'Not so, Lord, for I have never eaten anything that was common or unclean.' But you see – you can't say that. You can say 'Not so!', or you can say 'Lord,' but you cannot say both.

I want you to see Jesus as Lord of the Crisis. Now, there are some Christians who treat Him as if He were *only* the Lord of the Crisis, that is to say, they turn to Him only in the direct emergency, after they've tried everything else. After they've tried the church, the Pastor, the Bishop, the psychiatrist, the marriage-guidance counsellor, the family doctor, perhaps even (quietly) the horoscope column. Then, at last, defeated by their crisis, they turn to Jesus.

They are like the man who sent for a do-it-yourself kit for building a suite of furniture. When it arrived he struggled for hours and hours and worked himself into a frenzy, and to a point of near frustration. Whereupon his wife quietly handed him the little brochure that was included in the kit, and said, 'If all else fails, read the instructions.' There are far too many Christians who live that way. If all else fails – try Jesus. There are others, of course, who treat Him as if He were only Lord of other people's crises. He may be the answer to the crisis facing the missionary in Iran, or the neighbour in distress, or the sinner in his guilt, but not my crisis.

How wonderful it is to come across Christians who in their crises turn to the Lord. It has been my privilege to travel widely in Eastern Europe, and I've been to places (I wouldn't tell you where, because that wouldn't be wise) where the tension was tremendous. I remember one occasion when three men came to me and said 'We want to talk to you, we want to tell you some things.' So I said 'Where can we meet?' They said 'We can't tell you where to meet yet.' They were afraid they might be overheard. There might be a bugging device. Eventually on the Saturday morning, we met. Do you know where we met? We met in four feet of water in a thermal swimming pool. The idea was that if anybody was wearing a hearing device he would have to wear it above water level and we would see it. There are Christians who live with that kind of tension. But the remarkable thing about them, when you meet them, is their confidence and their expectancy of the Lord to be real in the crisis. To be honest, they put us to shame by their trust. If He is adequate for their crisis, why not for ours?

There are others who regard Him only as Lord of the *spiritual* crisis. So Jesus is not consulted in matters of crisis in your job, or your family, or among your friends – only in matters of 'spiritual' concern. Now the story in Mark 9 is a reminder that Jesus is Lord, and wants to be Lord, of the everyday, the personal, the domestic crisis. Here was a man demented by his son's illness – and he came to Jesus. Would that we could all learn, when we run into a family crisis, to come to Jesus; to bring our children – in their need, or sickness, or rebellion, or confusion – to Jesus. And I'm talking as the father of what to me are the two most precious youngsters in the world. They're in their teens. Believe me, long ago we entrusted them to Jesus.

Now there are three things about the crisis in this story we've read that I want you to see; very simply, and to begin with, I want you to recognise *the heartbreak of the crisis*. For this family, it was a terrible tragedy. They had a deaf and dumb child, a child retarded, possessed, disturbed, sometimes to the point of violence. There are few tragedies more pathetic. I remember in Glasgow many years ago, when I was a student sharing in the conducting of an evangelistic mission, going into a home where there was a woman in her fifties. Her husband lay in bed. He had been there many months with an acute heart condition. Sitting in a chair by the fireplace was a youngster, about seven years of age. She was strapped into a chair. She made no movement; when we went in, she didn't lift her head, she didn't look round. I couldn't take my eyes away from her. Her mother said softly, 'Don't worry; she has been like that all her life. In her entire life, she has never shown any recognition, never responded to any action, and now she's twenty-three years of age.' I shall never forget the sense of tragedy of that moment. But I'll tell you something else; I shall never forget, either, the immensity of that mother's triumph in that crisis, in which, simply and confidently and expectantly, she trusted Jesus to be Lord.

It may be that you have a domestic crisis. It may be in your own relationships, it may be in your family, it may be with your children. I want you to see that the one thing you can do with that crisis, heartbreaking as it may be, is to trust it to Jesus.

Do you remember the story of Elisha at Dothan, and his young companion? As they looked around them his companion was obsessed by the strength of the enemies. 'Elisha,' he said, 'we're done for, we're finished, there are enemies all around us.' And Elisha said, 'My boy, don't you see?' 'I can't see anything,' said the young man, 'except our enemies.' You know what Elisha did? He prayed. 'Lord,' he said, 'open the young man's eyes.' And God did. And he looked again, and this time he saw the hillsides thronging with the chariots of God.

Are you grieving over someone close to you who can only see the problems, and who cannot see what you see with the eye of faith? What are you going to do? Bully him? Argue with him? Reason with him? You can try all of these, but I urge you, above all else, pray for him! Let Jesus be Lord of that crisis, and trust Him with it.

Secondly, I want you to see *the hopelessness of the crisis.* You see, there was nothing they could do to put it right. In fact the problem became a source of dispute, and when Jesus arrived on the scene they were having a ding-dong argument about what to do next. Even the disciples could do nothing. The parents had told everybody that they had tried everything. And, sometimes, men and women in their crisis can find help nowhere, not among friends, lawyers, or even in church among the disciples. But Jesus is the Lord of the hopeless crisis.

I shall never forget a young man I met in Djakarta in Indonesia, nine years ago. I was preaching in an evangelistic crusade, and this man was the choir leader. He was a most attractive person. His choir did everything he asked of them. I saw him with a group of children, and they loved him. I spoke to the minister. 'Mike, tell me about this young man, he fascinates me.' The pastor said to me, 'Don't you know his story?' 'No,' I said. 'I don't know anything about him.' 'Well,' he said, 'that young man is a murderer.' 'Just a minute,' I said. 'I meant the choir leader.' 'So did I,' said the pastor.

And then he told me the most lurid story, of a boy brought up in a home where violence was the order of the day – he'd known nothing else. At the age of twelve he killed a boy in a brawl, and began a life of crime. By the age of eighteen he was serving a life sentence. He broke out of prison and killed the governor. Then he formed a band of brigands. He was caught and thrown into prison, in solitary confinement. He was there for many months.

One day, three men from the little church came to the prison. They asked to see all the prisoners, and eventually were shown into the solitary confinement cell. They told him of Jesus. He had never heard the name – his background was Buddhist – and he laughed them to scorn. 'Jesus? Who is He?' They went back, every week for three months – six months – nine months – one year – two years. Every time, they told him of Jesus, and he could not believe. 'What can anybody do with my life?' he said in despair. Then one day when they arrived he was waiting for them. 'Look,' he said, 'I don't understand this Jesus of yours, but if He can do anything with my life, let Him do it now.'

They knelt together and he invited Jesus Christ to come into his life: 'If You can do anything, do it now.' Today, that man is a full time preacher of the Gospel! Who did it? Jesus did it! The Lord of life's bitterest and most helpless crises.

And I want you to see, thirdly, *the handling of the crisis.* Because this father found his answer in Jesus as Lord. 'Lord, I believe, help Thou mine unbelief.' Now, those words tell you three simple things about Christ as Lord of the crisis. Firstly, lordship – not dependent on us, but established by God – *calls for a clear recognition of Jesus* – it's possible for Him to be Lord and for you not to recognise Him as such. This man calls Him Lord.

You can believe that Jesus is Lord, as a principle. With all our hearts we believe it, we sing a chorus sometimes 'He is Lord.' But there's another kind of belief, when you look Jesus in the eye and say, 'You are *my* Lord.' We need to move on from belief in a principle, to recognition of a Person. If you're to find Christ in life's crises, it will mean a clear encounter in which you recognise His lordship, in which you'll lay hold upon Jesus for yourself out of gratitude for the fact that on the cross, He laid hold upon you. When you discover Jesus as Lord, it brings the Eternal God, transformingly, consciously, right into your crisis. Look Him in the face, and make Him Lord!

And lordship calls for *complete reliance on Jesus.* 'Lord,' he said, 'I believe.' Now this was a real advance. At first his faith was so tentative. You can't blame him really. The lawyers and the disciples had done nothing; now he comes to Jesus: 'If you can do anything . . . ' The New International Version renders Jesus' reply like this: 'What do you mean, "If you can"?' You know, that's the trouble with so many of us. We're still at the 'If you can' stage with Jesus. But Jesus says, 'What do you mean?'

Everything is possible for him who believes. Not believes in himself, but in Christ. The power for meeting your crisis is not in yourself but in your Lord; but you'll never know it, unless you have faith enough to trust Him.

And finally, lordship calls for *a continual recourse to Jesus.* 'Help Thou mine unbelief.' Do you know, I'm glad he said that because it opens up the way for most of us, if we're honest. My friend, as you exercise trust in the Lord in your crisis, don't forget the devil will hit you hard with another if he has the chance. The person who takes his relationship to Jesus, and His lordship, seriously, is in the battlefield. There will be counter-attack. So you need to pray, with this man, 'Lord I believe, help Thou mine unbelief.' You see the lordship of Jesus is to be discovered and rediscovered daily. Before you go to other things, go to Jesus. In every new crisis there is a recourse to Jesus. Thus do we find sufficiency in place of struggle. The changeless element is Christ; the changeable element, me.

My brother, my sister, next time you're in a crisis, don't wait before trusting the Lord. Trust Him, in the crisis, and you will discover that He is not a disappointment.

'Lord, I believe, help Thou mine unbelief.'

THE SHEPHERD PSALM

by Rev. Keith Weston

66S105[6]

Psalm 23

In this psalm there are three statements made by the writer about himself, which are rich truths for everybody who knows Jesus as the Shepherd. In other words, when we surrender ourselves to the lordship of the Lord Jesus Christ, He enables us to make these glorious affirmations which nobody else can make. So here are my headings.

I shall not want – for He is the Lord of infinite grace;
I shall not worry – for He is the Lord of all wisdom;
I shall not wander – for, dwelling with Him, I shall be under His unerring leadership.

I think that's lovely. And I believe it may be a word to many of us, to surrender to the loving Lord who calls Himself 'The Good Shepherd'. And let us get rid of Satan's dreadful lie that if you yield yourself, body and soul, to Christ, it will be incalculable loss. It will not! It will be incalculable gain. Far from wanting to strip me of everything worthwhile in my life this Good Shepherd desires to clothe me in riches. 'I shall not want . . . I shall not worry . . . I shall not wander.' I will dwell with Him always.

So David makes his first affirmation, *'I shall not want.'* And I add as comment: because the Shepherd is Lord of all grace. A few psalms further on David says (Psalm 34:8)

'Those who seek the Lord lack no good thing.' And there are thousands of Christians who would say 'That is *my* experience, all down the years of my life.' Listen to Paul in Romans 8: 'Will He not also with Him give us freely all things?' And again that magnificent opening to the Epistle to the Ephesians: 'Blessed be the God and Father of our Lord Jesus Christ, who has blessed us in Christ with every spiritual blessing in the heavenly places.' Isn't it an astonishing statement? He *has* blessed us – already – with every spiritual blessing He has to give us. 'I shall not want,' for the lavish grace of my Saviour has made over to me, of all people, every spiritual blessing He has in the heavenly places in Christ. (And beware of 'writing your own version' – wanting to re-write that in your heart as 'Yes, thank you Lord; you have blessed me in Christ . . . with some niggardly things.' That's a wicked lie!)

If the Lord is your Shepherd, He has blessed you with every blessing and the call is to surrender yourself to the Lord, and enter into the fullness of those blessings. Go on all your earthly pilgrimage; go on over the grave; go on into all eternity. And you will not exhaust the riches that are yours in Christ. 'His divine power,' writes Peter, 'has granted to us all things that pertain to life and godliness.' All things!

What is your situation? You see, what spiritual truth lies behind this beautiful picture language: 'He leads me beside the still waters' – just exactly tailored to my need. He makes over His riches to me where I am now, in restoration of my soul, in leading me in the paths of righteousness day by day through this earthly life. For His name's sake.

As a Christian you are riding with the King of Kings. It's yours not to tag along, but to ride with Him. You're not there by mistake or presumption, but by His gracious and loving invitation, 'Sit here with Me.' He has blessed us in Christ with every spiritual blessing – in the heavenly places. 'I shall not want' – such love He sets on us. Do you perhaps feel the weakness and impoverishment of your spiritual life? Look to this Saviour, into His face, so that you can say, 'The Lord is my Shepherd, *I shall not want.*'

Secondly, *'I shall not worry.'* The Psalmist goes on to speak very realistically of experiences in life which may be yours or mine at any moment, perhaps even now. Commentators have often pointed out that the words 'of death' may not be in the original and it could be simply 'the valley of the shadows'. Of course of those shadows, the shadow of death is the one we shall all have to face if the Lord does not come back before we tread that valley. It's a very dark, perhaps difficult valley. None of us have gone that way before. But, 'I shall not worry,' said the Psalmist. Why? 'For Thou art with me.' Notice the change in pronoun – from 'He leads me . . . He feeds me . . . He makes me to lie down . . . ' but, when I get into the valley, the relationship is even closer – 'Thou art with me.'

There's a related passage in Psalm 84:5: 'Blessed are the men whose strength is in Thee, in whose hearts are the highways to Zion.' Blessed are those whose strength is in this gracious Lord, to whom they yield their lives, walking home to Zion – that is what possesses their hearts. But where does that pilgrim life lead them? Well, the Psalmist is again so true to life. Verse 6: 'As they go through the valley of Baca, they make it a place of springs.' A very dry and arid place, the 'Vale of Weeping', as Coverdale's version says. They go through what Psalm 23 would call 'the Valley of the Deep Shadows'. What do they do? Do they just mope away their days in the Valley of Baca? Do they turn bitter against the Lord and say, 'Why have you brought me here?' No, indeed not. Those who have committed their lives to the Lord Jesus are those who make the Valley of Baca a place of springs. They don't sit idle under sufferings, but, so to speak, they get their shovels out and dig wells, and they find the grace of God. 'They go from strength to strength,' and if the Lord had not led them on that path through the Vale of Weeping they would not have had their faith strengthened to come out the other side better than they went in.

What a strange truth; the Lord doesn't bring us into the valley to make us bitter, but to make us better. And how reassuring the end of verse 7 – 'The God of gods will be seen in Zion.' He doesn't let them go when they are in their misery and say 'Well, I've lost them, I'll look after somebody else.' No! 'Thou art with me, Thy rod and Thy staff are my comfort.' 'The God of gods will be seen in Zion' – in other words, He will bring you through, and you'll come out the other side tried but purified, for He knows the way I take. 'I shall not worry' – because He is the Lord of all wisdom who directs my life. Isn't that wonderful?

There are those even now who are going through the Vale of Baca. Maybe you're burdened as a Christian with problems almost too great to bear. I tell you, if the Lord is your shepherd, then you are safe in His hands and you need not fear. Entrust yourself to the Lord; He will see you through. Perhaps you are in a very lonely place of service, some factory floor where you are the only Christian, where you have been ostracised and ridiculed for months; or maybe you are a missionary, full of discouragement, full of problems, perhaps even difficult relationships with other missionaries. 'I shall not fear,' even in the hard places of the Lord's appointed service, 'for Thou art with me.'

And there are those among you who will soon be treading that final Valley of the Shadow of Death. And there is no fear there. I say that even on the authority of Scripture. 'For Thou art with me' – even there.

Thirdly, *'I shall not wander.'* You see he is speaking of a goodness and mercy following him all the days of his life and of the dwelling in the house of the Lord for ever. The Hebrew verb could well be a future as well as a present tense, and I see here a picture of a man or a woman who, all through the long and wearisome pilgrimage, dwells consciously in the presence of the Lord who spreads a table for him. The Lord is there, and he dwells with the King.

I shall not wander, because He is the Lord of unerring leadership, all the way home. And I love that too, for I feel the appalling weakness of my spiritual life more often than I dare say. I've heard it said that it's so appropriate that Isaiah says in the classic chapter 53, 'All we like sheep have gone astray.' And in the Shepherd's Psalm, it's like silly stupid sheep that we wander away. We like to think that we go astray like tigers or lions, that we assert our authority and snap our fingers at the Lord; no doubt that does sometimes characterise our rebellion. But most of the time we just go astray like silly sheep. There's nothing very frightening, is there, about a sheep? But a sheep can get frighteningly lost – and we wander away from the arms of the Shepherd more often than not.

But with the Lord as my Shepherd, how can I wander, with Him beside me and his sheepdogs Goodness and Mercy following me, all the days of my life? I shall dwell in his presence day by day. He is the dearest friend I have. As Paul says, we have peace with God through our Lord Jesus Christ, as we look back over the past which is gloriously blotted out by this Saviour. And we have access to this grace so that the present is covered and I shall not be bowled over by the circumstances of life. And what's more, looking ahead to the future I rejoice in my hope of sharing the glory of God guaranteed for me by the Shepherd who follows me all the days of my life until at long last I enter home.

These three great Christian affirmations all derive inexorably from the opening statement of the psalm which speaks of the lordship of Jesus. 'The Lord is my Shepherd.' If you know your Old Testament theology, you will understand that the word doesn't only speak of cuddly sheep and so forth, but of leadership of Israel. In Ezekiel 34, for example, the leaders are referred to as 'Shepherds of Israel.' So King David is therefore saying, 'The Lord is my King.' That's the thought that comes to mind for the Hebrew as he reads this psalm. And I say, I can only make these three great assertions provided my heart and life are surrendered to the kingship of the loving Shepherd.

Would you know the life that knows no want, no worry, no wandering? Then you must get on your knees, and surrender all authority and power in your life to this loving King.

LIVING UNDER CHRIST'S LORDSHIP

by Rev. David Jackman

John 13:1–17

There are few places in the New Testament where I find myself drawn nearer to the loving heart of the Lord Jesus than in the thirteenth chapter of John's Gospel, to which I invite you now to turn with me, as we consider what it means to live under the lordship of Christ.

You will be very familiar with the context of these verses. The disciples had come in from Bethany, to that hot and dusty upper room; and courtesy, or even duty, would have prompted one of them to perform the office of a servant in washing the others' feet. But Luke tells us in chapter 22 of his Gospel, that a dispute had arisen among them, as to which was the greatest. It may in fact have been triggered by this very situation. Or perhaps they were aware that a climax in our Lord's ministry was near, and they were concerned about who would hold the leading positions in the kingdom which He was to bring in. Either way, they had scarcely begun to understand the values of Christ's kingdom, or the nature of Christ's lordship. And it wasn't until the meal was under way, that our Lord Jesus rose, in order to perform the task that they had each had the opportunity of fulfilling, but had each refused. In doing so, He showed them a living example of what He meant, when He said: 'I am among you as one who serves.'

Look with me firstly then at *the Master's action* in these verses 1 to 5. The opening three verses state, almost incidently, the central fact; that is, the sovereign authority of the Lord Jesus Christ, who is at the centre of this picture. And then verses 4 and 5 illustrate in a most graphic way what that fact of Christ's lordship implies and involves. As you look at these verses, you will see how everything centres around the perfect knowledge of the Lord Jesus, and His resolute obedience to the Father's will. Verse 1: 'Jesus knew that the time had come for Him to leave the world and go to the Father.' Verse 3: 'Jesus knew that the Father had put all things under His power, and that He had come from God and was returning to God.'

He knew that the time was ripe; the hour had come. He knew when He was going to leave this world; when He was going to accomplish His exodus. No other man knows that. No other man speaks of his own death in that way. Jesus was sovereign over the whole situation. He knew where He was going. He was returning to the Father's right hand. He knew why He had come, because the Father had put all things under His power, and that power was to be demonstrated in His Victory on the Cross, over all the hostile forces that were opposed to God's will. And He knew where He had come from. He was from God and returning to God.

And John is also saying to us: He is in total control of this whole situation, as He always is, of every situation, because the Father with whom He is in perfect relationship, has put all things under His power. And that is the reality of life in this world and our Lord Jesus supremely knew it. Life and death, men and nations, all judgement, all things have been committed to the Son, and are under His control. And so the events that are about to happen – His betrayal, His humiliation, His death, His resurrection, His ascension to glory – all things are under His power.

And there is in a sense in these chapters in John a glorious inevitability about it from God's side. The Lord Jesus came to do the Father's will, perfectly and totally, until He could cry on the cross as He dismissed His Spirit, 'Finished!' And that great cry of victory which opened wide the gates of Heaven to receive the Lord, the Conqueror over sin and death and hell, was an expression of the perfect fulfilment of the will of the Father.

But there is also a wonderful submission and humility about it on the human side, and this is the thrust of the shock that I'm sure we are meant to feel as we come to verse 4. For this Lord Jesus who is sovereign over the whole situation – who has all things under His power, rises from the table. What for? To command his disciples to worship Him? To proclaim His lordship to them on the eve of His death? That's what we might expect to find, and in a sense it is what we find, but we discover it in what humanly speaking is the most unlikely manifestation of a sovereign's authority and rule.

He rose from the table in order to wash His disciples' feet. And here, in the full consciousness of His Messiahship, our Lord Jesus enacts for those He loves the meaning of His coming and His cross. Who is the greatest in the Kingdom of Heaven? The yardstick in His Kingdom is service.

He wrapped a towel around Him, He took the form of a servant, He began to wash His disciples' feet. He humbled Himself and became obedient. And this is not just a wonderful and moving picture of our Lord's humility, it is an illustration of His whole work, and it sets for us the ethos of His Kingdom. For isn't the root of human sin the pride and rebellion that we find in our own hearts against God?

When that temptation first came to Eve, and to Adam, it was couched in words that are highly significant. 'You shall be as gods, knowing good and evil.' And the root of sin is that I want to be my own god; I want to live life my own way; I want to be my own boss. And the only antidote to poison like that is a total obedience to the Father's will, which is shown here in an absolute humility. For when the Lord Jesus went to the cross, He was presenting there, not simply a pure body, not simply a life free from sin, but a perfectly obedient will to the Father, which He offered as a substitute for our rebellious and sinful wills.

Now you cannot grow that in this world's soil. It's got to come from somewhere else. It's got to come from another kingdom, where the greatest is the Servant of all, where love reigns, where the mark of the Lord is that He gives Himself in limitless love for His people. And if that sort of plant is to be nourished in our lives and in the unlikely soil of our hearts, then it is only possible when the King of Love Himself is enthroned in our hearts and lives. Then the mark of the reigning Lord Jesus will be seen.

But John takes us from the Master's action, to *Peter's objection* in verses 6 to 11. Peter often did his thinking aloud, like many of us, and you find in verse 8 that he blurts out, 'Lord! You? *My* feet? Never! It's all wrong, Lord.' Hadn't Simon Peter confessed this Man as the Lord of Glory? Hadn't he said, 'We believe that You are the Christ, the Son of the Blessed'? How unthinkable that the Lord of Glory should wash Peter's dirty feet. And Jesus replies to him, when He says in verse 6, 'Lord, are You going to wash my feet?' 'You do not realise now what I am doing (verse 7) but later you will understand. You don't know at the moment, Peter, the significance of this. Your mental processes don't enable you to grapple with it, and to understand it. You can't make it out at present, but you will perceive it later on. My future providences will explain to you what is a dark mystery in the present.' And when we find ourselves in that sort of situation, if we are really living under the lordship of the Lord Jesus, then the secret is to hold on to Him, and to be obedient to whatever He says, however dark the tunnel may be. That's what faith is. That's living under His lordship. But verse 8 is sheer pride, and self-confidence. 'No', said Peter, 'You shall never wash my feet.' It's a very strong negative. 'No, by no means will You ever, not in all Eternity, Lord, will You wash my feet.'

And Peter had to learn what we have to learn, over and over again, that you cannot say, 'No' and 'Lord' in the same breath. For Jesus Himself says, in the second part of verse 8, 'Unless I wash you, unless you submit to what I want to do in your life, you have no part with Me.' And we have to learn this over and over again, do we not? That in every practical issue, where the lordship of Christ challenges us to obedience, we are not in a position to object to His will for us. We cannot be His, and remain independent of His commands and His purposes. Either I allow the Lord to be Lord, and to do what He desires with my life, or, in effect, I walk out of fellowship with Him.

Sometimes we're very heroic about this. There's a lot of talk in Christian circles about being 'broken'. Sometimes it's rather glib talk. But we wouldn't have to be so heroic about the Lord breaking us, if we would humbly and progressively submit to His Lordship in all the little decisions. Being broken is really a matter – if it happens in our lives – of the Lord taking ultimate measures with us, because we will not let go of something that is quite worthless, but which in effect is saying, 'No, Lord', in our experience. You see, our part in Christ is entirely on His terms, and His terms are terms of unquestioning surrender and obedience.

But Peter, like us, is so slow to understand, and he says, when the Lord says to him, 'Unless I wash you, you have no part with Me', 'Then, Lord, not just my feet, but my hands and my head as well.' 'The larger the area washed, Lord, the greater the blessing, so bath me.' And Jesus replies, as we were reminded last evening, that there is an initial, once for all washing, experienced when we first come to Him, that's received from His hands, on His terms. But that every day, walking in the world, our feet are dirtied, sometimes they pick up grime, sometimes they deliberately walk into it. But that living under His Lordship means a daily cleansing, a daily submission, a daily reassessment, a daily willingness to receive all that the Lord wants to give me.

Finally then, notice with me in verses 12 to 17, *our own obligation.* Verse 12, the process of the foot-washing, is completed, and the Lord resumes His place, as He is soon to do in His heavenly glory. When He had finished washing their feet, He put on His clothes and returned to His place.

He's been showing to them His own unquenchable love, in this cleansing which He will die to provide. He's been giving them an example that they should follow in His steps. And verse 12 comes to us too, very personally. It's as though the Lord is saying to us, 'Do you understand what I've done for you? Well then!' (verse 14) 'Now that I, your Lord, have washed your feet, you ought always to be washing one another's feet!' And He is telling us that to live under the lordship of Christ, is to belong to a Servant/Master, whose love gives and gives, to the point of self-sacrifice. That is the life-style of His Kingdom. That is to be the hallmark of our citizenship. The Christian community is called by its Lord to be a foot-washing community, and if the Lord and Master loves you and me enough to perform such a supreme act of self-abasement, how dare we imagine that we have any dignity to stand on? We call Him Teacher and Lord. Why do we do that, if we do not also do what He commands us? That's the distinctive mark of living under His lordship.

As the chapter goes on to say in verse 34, 'A new commandment I give to you. Love one another; as I have loved you, so you must love one another. All men will know that you are my disciples if you have love one for another.' And it's that sort of caring, loving, self-sacrificing giving, that is a mark of the life in which Christ is Lord.

And you'll note the solemn words of verse 16: 'I tell you the truth. No servant is greater than his master, nor is the messenger greater than the one who sent him.' So that if I claim exemption from a life of self-giving love, I am in fact asserting that I am greater than my Lord. My privilege as a Christian is to be sent on His errands, as He chooses. Our privilege is to submit ourselves exclusively and entirely to the great Sender, and the ministry of our Lord Jesus Christ is the pattern of all true Christian service. He stooped to conquer. Living under His lordship, means being at His disposal, to serve in whatever way He directs. But that sort of humility doesn't characterise us enough as God's people. Sometimes we are too aware of other people's imperfections, but we don't want to wash their feet. Or we are so self-centred, that if a brother would come to wash our feet, we angrily withdraw them.

One of our hymns puts it very cogently, when it says, 'a life of self-renouncing love, is one of liberty', and to live under His lordship is to follow His example. Again, years later, Peter was to write in his first Epistle, (5:5), 'Clothe yourselves with humility towards one another.' It's the only New Testament usage of a verb meaning to put on a slave's costume, to take upon yourself the garb of the servant. Do you not think his mind was back in that upper room? And he was saying to those Christians, as he says to us, 'You don't judge; you don't withdraw; you serve, if you are living under His lordship.' It was a lesson that Peter learned progressively, by doing it. And verse 17 highlights that very fact. It isn't a promise, it's just a plain statement of fact. Now that you know these things you will be blessed if you do them. Happiness, blessing, fulfilment, comes through action. To live under Christ's lordship is to be committed to the Servant/Master, to a life of foot-washing, and to discover in that self-giving, the happiness which is nowhere else. 'You call me Teacher', He says. 'Are you really learning? Learning to be like Me. Learning to follow in My pathway. Not simply learning about Me, or filling your mind with My truth, but working it out in practice. You call Me Lord. Are you truly obedient to what I'm telling you?' Are you prepared to go back to the foot-washing; to keep on serving; to be led into new areas of service which may be very costly and very challenging? Is our Christianity just words, or is it reality? Because if we are going to live under His lordship, we've got to be available to serve wherever He sends us. And if we live like that, then we shall become increasingly like the Lord Jesus. And that's what the world needs to see.

That's living under His lordship. And He says to us tonight, 'Now that you know these things, you will be blessed, you will be blessed, if you do them.'

HOW FULLNESS SERVES

by Rev. George Duncan

Acts 6

I want to study with you the character of the man called Stephen who is described as a man *full* of the Holy Ghost. We are living in days when much prominence is being given to the Person, and to at least one of the gifts, of the Holy Spirit. I want to learn from the life and work of one man, concerning whom we are not told that he possessed that particular gift, but concerning whom we *are* told three times that he was full of the Holy Ghost.

In Acts 6:4 the men that were to be chosen to help in the expanding and growing work of the Church were to be men full of the Holy Ghost. In verse Stephen is described as such a man. A man *full* of faith and of the Holy Ghost. He was not only spoken of as full of the Holy Ghost, but full of much else besides. In verse 3 – full of wisdom; in verse 5 – full of faith, or maybe faithfulness; in verse 8 – full of grace (so the RSV translates the word faith); and full of power. Actually we don't find the word the 'fullness' of the Holy Spirit, we find the fullness of God, but it is simply the noun form of the adjective used to describe being full of the Holy Spirit and of the verbal form that we find elsewhere in Scripture. The significant thing to me is that when Stephen is first mentioned and when he is last mentioned (7:55) he is described as being full of the Holy Ghost. A man in whose life that fullness was maintained right to the end.

Let's see what, in his life, it meant to be full of the Holy Ghost. I wonder whether that could be said of you or of me, that you are a man or woman full of the Holy Ghost? It ought to be possible to say it if we have obeyed the command to be continually being filled with the Holy Spirit. The Holy Spirit: that source of power promised by the risen Lord on the ascension mount when He said 'You shall receive power after that the Holy Ghost is come upon you, and you shall be witnesses unto Me unto the uttermost parts of the earth'. Stephen, the man who lived a life of maintained fullness right to the end, who lived at the floodtide. Now as I was reading over the life of this man, and noticing this phrase 'full of the Holy Ghost', I found three characteristics of his life which seemed to me are bound to be characteristics of the life that is lived at floodtide.

1. How fullness serves

The Holy Spirit is called in Romans 8:9 'the Spirit of Christ', and you will recall how Christ said of Himself in Luke 22:27 when the disciples were quarrelling amongst themselves as to which of them should be accounted the greatest, 'I am among you as He that serveth.' And Stephen is presented to us first of all, in all his fullness of the Spirit of God, as one who is called to serve the Church. That's the very first thing. And of course when you and I realise that with the new life of the Spirit of God has come the very love of God into our lives and that love is always active and love always longs to serve, we can understand how a life that is full of the Holy Ghost will be a life that is a serving life. You remember how Paul in Romans 5:5 says 'the love of God has been shed abroad in our hearts by the Holy Ghost who has been given to us.' Now note exactly what Paul says: 'the *love* of God has been shed abroad in our hearts'. And with the new life there came the new love. Indeed John adds his testimony 'in this way we will know that we have passed from death unto life'. How? Because we love. The new love is the evidence of the new life. So what is the distinctive mark of love? Surely it longs to serve, to work, to toil, to do things for those it loves. Love is never idle, never inactive. And so Paul can write again in 2 Corinthians 5:14, 'the love of Christ constraineth us' – compels us.

I feel I must pause to define what we mean by love for just a moment. This Christian love is agapé love. It would seem as if the Spirit of God had to find a new word to describe the quality of love which is distinctively the divine love, which is the fruit of the Spirit. And the word used is the word *agape*, different from both erotic love and natural affection. My Greek dictionary describes and defines it as a reverential love. It is a love which is not so much something to do with being fond of, as recognising the worth of, the value of, the importance of, a person. Agapé love is concerned with how important is that person to me. Not, do I give them a kiss maybe, but how much time do I give them? And how much does their life matter to me? How much do they matter to me? That is agapé love. A minimum of emotion, but a maximum of evaluation. I want to clarify this because when we are thinking how fullness serves, it is the motivation of this agapé love, the love of God, not our knowledge of the love of God, but the very love of God, the very same quality of love, the very love itself of God has been shed abroad in our hearts by the Holy Spirit.

And as we watch how fullness serves in the life of this man, I just want to note two things. First of all: *the lowliness of the service asked of him*. It was initially to count the collection. Now that wasn't a very big job for a man to be asked to do. And then to make certain that the widows were being cared for. What a neglected and sometimes undervalued and under-rated section of society are the widows! This was the huge responsibility laid upon this extremely gifted and talented man. To count the collection and to go round and just see how the widows were getting on. You wouldn't have thought that was much of a job, would you? And here was a man who was humble enough, and willing enough, to do a very insignificant thing, by human standards, not by God's. And when you and I stop to think of it, listed in the various facets of this agapé love named by Paul in Galatians as the fruit of the Spirit, is included meekness. It's the same word as that used by Christ in the Sermon on the Mount; 'Blessed are the meek for they shall inherit the earth.' 'Gentleness' is the RSV rendering. I think it is really a blending of the two ideas of humility and gentleness, giving us a picture of what it is to be held in you. Not a spirit of aggression, self-assertiveness, self-promotion, but a gentle, kindly, gracious self-affacement. All I know is that the service that love renders is always a willing service to meet a need, to please the heart of someone cared for.

I believe that one of the tragedies of so much service is that we are willing to serve if the job is big enough for us. Stephen began in the back seat. I wonder if you are prepared to begin in the back seat. Do you think you are too big to take a Sunday School class? Are you too big for God to use? So while, after the service, the apostles would be busy talking to people coming up to them saying 'Thank you for that message' and all the rest of it, where was Stephen? Oh, he was in a back room counting the collection. That wasn't much of a job, was it? But that's where he started.

Then, *the faithfulness in service showed by him.* I am quite certain that if you and I were looking for somebody to carry out a responsibility one of the first things I would certainly look for would not necessarily be whether they were full of faith, or even full of the faith. I would look for somebody who was completely reliable, and completely dependable, and full of faithfulness. In the list of the different aspects of that love which is the fruit of the Spirit, we find a word that's translated 'faith' in the Authorised Version and translated 'faithfulness' in the RSV. And I am sure the RSV is right here, for the Holy Spirit is called again and again the Spirit of God. Surely one of the great characteristics of our God is His faithfulness, His total reliability, His utter dependability. Faithfulness for Stephen unto death. How fullness serves!

What is your objective when you are crying to God that you might know a fuller, deeper measure of the infilling of the Spirit of God? What are you wanting? I tell you what God wants. He is wanting to see in your life how fullness serves. And one of the things is the faithfulness in the service showed by you. God is faithful, reliable, dependable, and if the Spirit of God is in me in His fullness then the nature of that faithfulness and of that faithful God will be seen in me. I'm not interested, as the Pastor, in what people claim, what gifts they say they've got, what experiences they claim. I'm only concerned about one thing and that is, am I seeing the fruit of the Spirit in their life, and if I'm not then I'm concerned that there is something wrong in spite of all the claims made. How fullness serves. Isn't this tremendous? Stephen's faithfulness was costly. It cost him his life. How fullness serves! The lowliness of the service asked, the faithfulness in the service shown. God has a delightful way of doing the most extraordinary things through the tiniest little job.

2. How fullness speaks

Acts 6:10, 'They were not able to resist the wisdom and the spirit' – and I notice that in the New International

Version the word Spirit is printed with a capital 'S'. That's interesting, isn't it? They were not able to resist the wisdom and the Spirit by which he spake. The witness that Stephen was to give not simply with his life of service but with his lips was another way in which this man was outstanding. Look at what he said. Two things emerge. First,

The insights that he had into the truth of God. So important was this aspect of his contribution to the life of the Church that fifty-three verses in the seventh chapter are given over to recording what he said. Here was a man who was absolutely soaked in the scriptures. A man who was deeply taught by the Spirit. And I want to suggest to you that one of the great ministries of the Holy Spirit is His teaching ministry. And this is a ministry that He's been given to exercise in the life of every believer. This has nothing whatever to do with the gift of teaching which He gives to some but not to all. But this is a ministry and there is all the world of difference between the ministries of the Holy Spirit and the gifts of the Holy Spirit. The ministries are the things He wants to do, and He wants to do them in all believers. The gifts he gives differently. You remember how Jesus said in John 14:26; 'He will teach you', John 16:13; 'He will guide you into all truth'. Paul writing to the Ephesians in 1:17 prayed 'that God may give you the spirit of wisdom and revelation in the knowledge of Him'. This is a ministry that the Holy Spirit wants to exercise in your life. He wants you to be deeply taught in the things of God. He doesn't want you to have an 'A' level or a degree in theology, He just wants you to graduate in the University of Heaven.

You know you often hear that verse quoted: 'Eye hath not seen, nor ear heard, neither have entered into the heart of man the things that God hath prepared for them that love Him'. Now that is all referred to Heaven. Well, of course, it applies to Heaven, but it doesn't just apply to Heaven. Paul goes on; 'but God has revealed them to us by His Spirit'. There is a whole realm of realities, principles, standards, insights, and God wants to teach you. Here was a man with wonderful insights into the truth of God. And when Christ promised the power of the Spirit so that the Christian would witness to Him, I am sure this was included in the promise because a witness knows what he is talking about.

The Holy Spirit will be our Teacher. This means we have to spend time in the classroom. How long do you spend with your Bible? We're going to become enlightened, instructed, informed. Compare what the average Christian knows about his faith, with what the average Communist knows about his. Compare that, honestly. Then can you wonder that the Communist cause is making progress? They know what they are talking about. But you and I don't. Some of us couldn't even tell somebody else how to become a Christian. We couldn't. That's a scandal and a disgrace if we've been Christians for any length of time. The Holy Spirit wants to teach you, and *the* Book comes first, and then other books. (Make certain that the writer is, not necessarily someone who is well-known, but somebody who is biblical and you can trust. Try different writers. One man's meat is another man's poison. You'll find some help you, some don't.) But become instructed, have insights, understand what you believe so that you can share it. And then,

The impact he made. They were not able to resist the wisdom and the Spirit by which he spake. And if we take that capital 'S' and put it in there we realise that the power behind his words was not Stephen's, it was the Spirit's power. The constraining power of the Spirit would tug at the hearts of men. The convicting power of the Spirit would grip the consciences of men. The transforming power of the Spirit would change the lives of those that obey.

One of the tremendous facts about the life and work

of the Holy Spirit is that He could use the simplest words, the most ordinary people, to do the most extraordinary things. You see you don't need to be a speaker at Keswick to be used of God. You don't need to be a great preacher, you can have your fireside chair with your tea-pot in your hand and your neighbour in front of you. You can live in a lodging somewhere in London, or in a hostel at a university or a hospital, and just invite one of your nurse friends, your fellow students to come in just for a chat; and the Holy Spirit, the power of the Spirit, can go through those words on your lips to change lives. That's the way God's ordained it. We talk about the sovereignty of God – that's how God's sovereignty is planned to work. I think it's tremendous. Not all will receive, of course. Some may resent. Under conviction one either repents and believes or becomes angry, and persecutes.

3. How fullness shines

Acts 6:15: 'All that sat in the council looking steadfastly on him saw his face as it had been the face of an angel'. The word I want us to take and grip is 'all the Council looking on him *saw*'. I've always been challenged by the way in which John in his Gospel and in his first Epistle underscores the visible as well as the verbal aspects of the Gospel. In John 1:14 he writes, 'The Word became flesh and dwelt among us', and he doesn't go on to say 'and we *heard*' but he goes on to say 'the Word became flesh and dwelt among us and we *beheld* His glory, the glory as of the only begotten of the Father, full of grace and truth'. And in 1 John 1:1; 'that which we have heard, which we have *seen*, and which our hands have handled of the Word of Life'. And all the Council *looking on him* steadfastly *saw* his face, the face of an angel. How fullness shines! What do people see when they look at you and they look at me?

I want just to note two things as we close. First of all, *the proximity in which that glory shone*. How close these men were to Stephen, just feet away. There they were, there this man was, and they looked at him at close range like that and his face was transformed. 'The Word became flesh' writes John 'and dwelt among us'. John had been rubbing shoulders with Jesus for three years, day and night, and said 'the Word became flesh and dwelt among us and we beheld the glory'. I tell you I want to suggest that it is in the closer relationships of life that the crunch comes. What do people see? Members of your family, what do they see? Your fellow workmates in the office, what do they see? The patients in the ward, what do they see? The pupils in the classroom, what do they see? Oh, we can talk, but what do they see? The tremendous thing about Naomi's impact upon Ruth was that in this close relationship of mother-in-law/daughter-in-law – notoriously difficult – Ruth couldn't resist the attraction of what she saw in her mother-in-law. 'I want your God to be my God'. Now tell me this, when people look at you, do they see anything that would make them want your God?

And finally, *the divinity of which the glory spoke*. Here was something that could only be described as supernatural. They saw his face as the face of an angel. Concerning our Lord, 'the Word became flesh and dwelt among us and we beheld His glory, the glory of the only begotten of the Father, full of grace and truth'. Martin Luther said very daringly, but quite truly, 'Every Christian is a miniature Christ.' The Word has become flesh again in you and in me. Do they see the glory?

This is a man full of the Spirit. And these are his characteristics: how he served, how he spoke, how he shone. And somehow or other those three hallmarks to me are much more likely to be hallmarks of the genuine fullness of the Holy Spirit than many of the things I hear tossed around and talked about today. Jesus said 'By their fruit ye shall know them'. And the fruit of the Spirit is love.

Full of the Holy Ghost – a man who lived at the flood-tide. I want to live there, don't you? And to live a life in which that fullness is maintained to the very end.

THE STRENGTHENING OF HIS SPIRIT

by Rev. Michael Baughen

Ephesians 3:14–21

Let me begin with an introduction. There are three things within this introduction. First thing; *your heavenly Father is never satisfied.* He loves you and me so much He longs for us to grow and grow towards the sort of people we could be for Him as part of His family. If you are a parent you know that's true of your own children. There is no point in saying 'That's it, they are perfect.' And if a child says to you 'Well, I'm not going to bother with my homework tonight, I've done enough to get through tomorrow and pull the wool over the teacher's eye' – well, you get worried if you are a parent. So how does your Heavenly Father feel, if you as a Christian cannot really be bothered to be the best for Him? Paul begins this prayer by showing us how much the Father cares. It's the Father who heads His family to whom this prayer is addressed and it's a prayer for grace.

But secondly, by way of introduction, as you look at this prayer, you will see that *your Heavenly Father wants you to receive more and more.* Verse 16: 'from the riches of His glory'. Now we know those are the inexhaustible riches of our God, so why is it that many Christians live in semi-poverty in their spiritual life? There are an awful lot of Christians whose Christian lives are merely polite tea-and-sandwiches, and God's banqueting table is laid out and they never partake; never want to. They are quite content to stagger along with their little bit of Christianity when all the riches of God are not only *available*, but the Father *wants* us to partake. Instead we go on with our little meetings, our little churchy concerns; and all the challenge, the grace, the power, the inspiration, the daring, the conviction, the understanding that is available from our Heavenly Father is hardly touched at all. Your Heavenly Father wants you to receive from the riches of His glory.

Thirdly, *your Heavenly Father expects you to ask.* There's nothing automatic about His bestowing the riches of His glory upon you; after all, the relationship, as this prayer makes clear, is between a Father and His children. And so this prayer is one of several prayers in the New Testament that goes straight to the Father and asks for spiritual growth. These prayers in the New Testament are concerned about the power of God in our lives, the love of God in our lives, the fullness of God in our lives and our service of God with our lives. Now let me ask you a straight question. When did you pray to God like that? When did you last pray to God for real spiritual growth in power, in love and usefulness in His service? I think it's probably true that with quite a lot of us this does not figure much in our prayer life. We pray for the conversion of the neighbour next door and the person in the office and the other person in the school or the college, but how much do you pray for spiritual growth in your own life, and then in the life of your fellow Christians, perhaps your pastor, or missionaries on the mission field? Now you alone can answer that question but I can tell you that if you mean business with the living God it should be on your prayer list every day. Why don't we? Why is it, that it is probably true that a large number of us do not pray very much like this at all?

If you don't pray for spiritual growth the only reason is that you are not interested, you couldn't care less, you are quite smug and satisfied with your spiritual life as it is now. 'Thank you very much – I'll just pray for my neighbour's conversion.' Is that true? My prayer is that if it's true of you, that God will meet you by His Spirit, and make you hunger and thirst to grow and begin to pray as the New Testament tells us to pray.

Well there are two main parts to the prayer, and the first part, in verses 16 to 17, is *prayer for power.* The power is inward strengthening. If you've got the RSV it says 'might' but the word means 'power', through His Spirit in the inner man. The NIV takes it on; 'so that Christ may dwell in your hearts by faith'. Now let's look at this; firstly, see that this is not a second experience, it isn't a dramatic extra to conversion or a receiving of the Spirit; the word is 'strengthening', strengthening by His Spirit. Strengthening, therefore, by He who clearly already indwells us. After all, we cannot be Christians without being indwelt by the Spirit of God – it makes us the Sons of God. But then grasp the wonder of it; look at this passage, think about it, there's a lot that we can do to grow. There's the discipline of reading and studying the Word of God, there's the discipline of prayer, there's the discipline of reading. I hope you read. Let your bookshelf reflect whether you mean business with God. There's much we can do in the training of our abilities and the gifts that God has given us. There is much we can do in listening and obeying and buffeting our body.

Before I was at theological college one person there believed God was going to call him as a missionary and he used to go out in the snow with a bathing costume on and roll in the snow to toughen himself up for missionary service. Now that man meant business with God. He is still on the mission field. There's a lot that we can do, but the superb truth of this verse is that this is matched by God's work in us. Let it hit you again. It is impossible for it to happen by anything that you do – only God can come within and influence you from within. It makes all the difference in the world between putting ointment *on* something and something *from within* to heal. There is nothing like this in the whole world; there is no other religion, no other philosophy, nothing, in which the living God can come into your human frame in personal indwelling. It is only possible in Christ by the work of the Holy Spirit. Notice it is a personal indwelling. Chapter 4:30 talks about our grieving the Spirit. You do not grieve a force or a thing. Now He does that, He indwells you for strengthening. Why? He indwells you for strengthening if you ask for it, that's the force of the prayer, isn't it – if you pray, if you long for it. Now see that this is the work of strengthening with power. The word 'strengthening' means 'makes strong'.

There are different ways in the New Testament of describing this. I want to give you just four. First there is *strengthening in witness*. For instance, Acts 4:31. The disciples are exhausted, they come back to God and pray, and they are refilled with the Holy Spirit. You know this, don't you? I hope you do. It's His ability to give you boldness. And second, *strengthening against the devil*. See Ephesians 6:10. Be strong in the Lord! God takes the battle seriously, He warns us, He tells us what armour to wear. The Holy Spirit can enable a man or a youngster to stand in the strength of God – if we ask! Then, thirdly, we see in Colossians 1:11 *strengthening in endurance*. It's true of St Paul who faced persecution so many times. As it's been said, Paul's body was the theatre in which Christ's glory was displayed. He dares to pray 'that I might know Christ and the power of His resurrection and may share His sufferings.' Here's a man who knows the strength of the Holy Spirit to endure.

The fourth area of strengthening is *triumph in weakness or suffering*. Some of you face problems that go on and on. And nobody will deny that in many cases the burden has gone on for years, and it's wearing you down. Well, Christ's power is made perfect in weakness; pray for the indwelling of the Holy Spirit. Isn't it marvellous that God wants to strengthen us in that way?

Then comes the great surprise of this passage. As you pray for this strengthening of the Holy Spirit, the experience that you are conscious of (verse 17) is that Christ is dwelling in your heart through faith. The Trinity is not divided, and it's one of the beautiful parts of the Holy Spirit that He glorifies Jesus. As He strengthens and renews and upholds us, He manifests Jesus. Wonderful!

But then the other part of the prayer is the manifestation of God's love. The prayer is not only that we might have power, but also *it is a prayer for love*. Now, you can have some of the gifts, but God expects you to have all of the fruit. And love, in passages like this, is often a shorthand for 'fruit of the Spirit'. God is concerned that we should mature in His love. Are we maturing? Now the Holy Spirit helps us to understand this. In Romans 5:5 we see that God's love – not ours for Him, but His for us on Calvary – has been poured into our hearts through the Holy Spirit. Do we go on being thrilled by Calvary? It is this passage's affirmation; we are *rooted* in love, nourished in love, like a tree.

And we are *grounded* in love, secure and immovable, like a building. When we cry, 'Abba, Father,' it is the Spirit bearing witness with our spirit that we are the children of God. Rooted, grounded; the Holy Spirit is constantly reaffirming it.

And (verse 18) He wants to take us on, to teach us more and more. To discover the wonder of that love. To apply it to our lives. To see love pouring out from us in patience and kindness and all those fruits we see in 1 Corinthians 13. He wants us to 'comprehend' that, and then He adds a plus to that comprehension; the growing, thrilling understanding of the love of God. It thrills us and humbles us and reduces us to silence.

Oh, it doesn't go on always. From time to time God manifests His love like this, wraps His arms around us and overwhelms us with the experience of love. Yet the experiences, perhaps, come and go. But this is what He wants to do for you; He wants you to have the fullness of God. He wants you to be filled. He aims at the best, and wants you and me to aim at the best also, so that He might be glorified.

And this is what the last two verses of the passage promise (verses 20 to 21). Do you know what the word 'abundantly' means? Paul uses the word *perisseuo*, and that means 'overflowing' – like a glass of water running over. But in Greek you can add things. You can put EK in front to make it a real cascading overflow. But the Holy Spirit isn't content with that, He put a *huper* in front – *huperekperrissou* – and the whole thing is going over the top like Niagara! That is the promise of God to you, says Paul. What limits it? We do. Many Christians limit the work of God by limited thinking and fixed views.

Don't you believe in a dynamic Holy Spirit who challenges us about our strategy, the way we go forward? All He wants us to do is stand back for the Director of the church, and say, 'Lord, am I stopping what You want to do in this church and this area?'

So I plead with you, and I ask you – I pray it myself – that if you mean business with the living God, start praying and praying and praying, that you may be strengthened with His power more and more. That you might be overflowed with the love of God in Christ. That you might be so part of the church submitted to His leadership that all He wants to do in that overflowing promise may not be limited by you, but that you might want to share in it with your life, your commitment, your gifts and the love of an overflowing heart; a heart that longs for the glory of Christ Jesus in the church and to all generations, for ever and ever.

THE GENERAL MISSIONARY MEETING

Oswald Sanders

Esther 4:14

A few days ago Michael Griffiths asked me, 'When were you last at the Keswick Convention?' I said, 'In 1947.' And then he asked, 'Do you realise that since then the population of the world has almost doubled?' And then he referred to a report stating that missionary recruitment in Britain over the past five years had dropped by forty per cent. I felt what a startling and serious comment it was on the contemporary missionary situation. Twice as many people in the world to be reached – and almost half the missionary force to reach them! If I said nothing else than that, I think that there is sufficient to present to us a tremendous challenge.

With that as background, I give my text: Esther 4:14. '. . . And who knows whether you have not come to the kingdom for such a time as this?'

The context was that the unscrupulous Haman had determined that he would destroy, not only the righteous Mordecai, but the whole Jewish nation in Persia (at that time, about 5,000,000 people). By a big bribe he secured the king's consent to destroy the nation. When Mordecai heard this terrible news he urged Esther, the Jewish consort of the king, to intervene on behalf of her nation. But apparently she had been out of favour, and the rule was that if a person – unless summoned – entered the king's presence, certain death would follow. And this verse was the climax of Mordecai's appeal to Esther. 'Who knows whether you have not come to the kingdom for such a time as this?' He was urging her to take this awesome risk, and maybe at the cost of life itself, to intervene.

Now it's implied that this was *an urgent and a critical hour;* 'such a time as this'. Did ever a young woman face a greater crisis? On one hand the certainty of terrible tragedy, on the other, the possibility of a glorious deliverance. And the whole thing hung upon her decision.

And what of our time? On one hand, we live in a time of upheaval; revolution, political, social and intellectual ferment, economic instability, moral chaos, spiritual decline. I wonder if any other generation has ever faced the same problems in their complexity and greatness as those of our generation. It doesn't take any vivid imagination, in our day at any rate, to imagine a tremendous economic collapse, or nuclear holocaust. Little wonder that the historian Toynbee likened our world to a canoe on the brink of Niagara.

On the other hand, what an exciting and challenging time to live in! In no realm is it more exciting than that of missions. For the first time it can be truly said that the church is universal. It couldn't be said in my youth; it can be said today. There really is no significant nation where the gospel flag has not been planted. Most of the lands of the world today are still open to the gospel. We talk about 'closed lands' – but what land is closed to prayer? To the working of the Holy Spirit? To the ministry of national Christians? To radio? To literature? All we can say is that the land is closed to western missionaries or to certain types of missionaries. God is at work in the 'closed lands'. Take China – only recently we have been hearing tremendously encouraging reports. One French pastor went comparatively recently to Hunan province, and he found seventy churches that used to be linked with the China Inland Mission, and they were still functioning. Not in big church buildings and not very openly, but one of them had two hundred members. Seventy churches still functioning! I heard of another province where, in many of the villages, there are only two or three families that are not Christian. They may be closed in one sense; but they are open in another.

And then, think of the tremendous strategy of the Holy Spirit in preparing receptive populations for the gospel all over the world. We've heard of Africa, we've heard of Latin America and the way God is working there. In Latin America today, I was told, there are 5,000 new churches coming into being every year. 100 new churches a week. And the same would be true of Africa. In 1959 there were 20,000,000 Christians south of the Sahara. Today there are 50,000,000 – almost one-third of the people. By the year 2,000 it is anticipated that the area will be fifty per cent Christian. You know, it's a tremendous challenge to us, in our favoured lands, as we see our brothers and sisters going out and winning their own people and the church growing.

I remember Bishop Festo Kivengere saying that in his diocese he had 850 churches with membership from 200 up to 2,000. And he said, 'Every year we add fifteen new churches to our diocese.' There are receptive populations growing up in different countries. In Latin America the population growth is three per cent; the growth of the Evangelical Church is ten per cent.

Any young or middle-aged man or woman who wants his or her life to count for God can have tremendous opportunities in many of these countries. It's estimated that by the year 2,000 there will be more Christians in the Third World than in the Old World. The centre of gravity is shifting. And we as Christians need to be concerned, lest the lampstand be moved because we are failing to rise to our responsibilities. Yes, there is tremendous receptivity. But the tragedy is that receptivity wanes. The harvest comes to ripeness – and then we lose it. I believe that now is the time for us to gird up our loins afresh, and take up this great task of taking Christ to the nations.

God is not going to be defeated by our lethargy, and one of the most wonderful and cheering things today is the birth of a new missionary force in the world. The strategy of the Holy Spirit is seen in the rise in missionary recruitment in the Third World. There are now very nearly 5,000 missionaries doing cross-cultural missionary work from those countries. The Japanese church aims by 1985 to send out 1,000 missionaries. The IVF of Japan has already sent out 100. The Korean church is aiming to send out thousands of missionaries by the year 2,000 – they're preparing for it. Here are nations with a vision! What is the vision of your church? How many people are you praying God will send out from your church? Are you praying that God will thrust out members of your church to go to the mission field? That's what the Lord said: 'Pray ye therefore the Lord of the Harvest, that He will thrust forth labourers into His harvest.' There are unparalleled opportunities today. Our own mission has a hundred openings we could fill tomorrow if there were people to fill them with, and this is the same in many parts of the world. The role of the missionary is undoubtedly changing. But for a person who is humble enough to work alongside and under nationals' leadership there are more strategic opportunities than ever before.

Now a word to those who are younger. U Thant called Asia and the Third World 'continents that have grown phenomenally young'. Who are the people responsible for the evangelisation of the youth of that generation? I'll tell you – the youth of *this* generation; and that means you! More than half the world is under twenty-one years of age. An entirely new situation. Short-term missionary work has done quite a bit, and it's valid, though limited. It will never on its own overtake the task that we face with the burgeoning population of the world. It takes time to learn the language, to absorb the culture of the people, to win their affection, to help the Christian church mature. It takes time. It takes people who will give themselves and their lives to this task.

It is for this that I appeal. The youth of this world for the youth of this generation. And older people: if I may say so, I began my missionary career at fifty-two, and my wife had her fiftieth birthday the night we left. There are many young or middle-aged men and women who could lay their gifts and experience at the feet of the Lord and find a tremendously rewarding sphere of service in many countries in the world. At a meeting I conducted in America, an old lady of seventy heard the call of God; she went down to Brazil and did three years of missionary work. When she finished that, she went to New Guinea and put in seven years of missionary work and then retired at eighty. So here's something for the older people too. Why shouldn't God have something for the older people? 'Such a time as this.' Who knows whether *you* have not come to the kingdom for such a time as this?

Mordecai impressed upon Esther *her position of unique privilege*. 'You've come to the kingdom.' Is it by chance that the Queen was a Jewess, the only one who had influence and might avert the massacre? And what about *our* unique privilege, my brothers and sisters? What nation is more privileged than we are? Oh, what we have! Our open Bible, our freedom to worship, our abundant Christian literature, our knowledge of salvation, our message . . . why has God given us these privileges? That we might hoard the bread of life? No, indeed. He's brought us to the kingdom 'for such a time as this'.

Mordecai further stressed to Esther *her personal and*

exclusive responsibility. 'You, Esther, you alone have been called . . . ' And I would like to say, 'You, *you*, have come to the kingdom. God has got some special contribution which you can make to the missionary cause, and nobody else in the world can make it. Are you prepared to do it?' I like J. B. Phillips' translation of Romans 1:14: 'I feel myself under a sort of universal obligation. I owe something to all men, from cultured Greek to ignorant savage.' That is the extent of your responsibility and mine. I owe something to all men, and I want as God helps me to discharge that responsibility.

One more thing, Mordecai pressed upon Esther *the necessity for personal involvement.* 'If you keep silent . . . you and your father's house will perish.' One of our maladies in our generation is that we don't like getting too deeply involved. But what is God asking of us? Not a cautious investment of our time and talents. He's saying that we are to present our bodies 'a living sacrifice' – for richer, for poorer, in sickness or in health, in life or in death, this is what God is asking. Not just a limited investment of a few pounds; but a pouring out of life in intercession, and, if necessary, in going and in pouring out our wealth too – there needs to be more sacrificial giving if the missionary task is to be completed. This is what God is asking of us. A living sacrifice.

Sir Frederick Treeves, the great British surgeon, knelt beside a wounded engine driver when the train on which he had been a passenger had had a terrible accident. He felt the man's body with his clever surgeon's hands, and then he rose and walked away. Those who were standing by heard him say this: 'I could have saved him – if only I had my instruments.'

My dear friends, as God looks down on this world of 4,000,000,000 people, of whom 2,500,000,000 have never yet come into vital contact with the Gospel, I believe

He's saying, 'I could save them – if only I had my instruments.'

Will you be His instrument, in 'such a time as this'?

After Dr Sanders' address, Canon Neech concluded the meeting with the customary invitation for people to stand in public commitment, if they wished to commit themselves to the mission field.

KESWICK CONVENTION 1979

List of tape numbers for addresses included in this book:

Rev. Alec Motyer, Bible readings

1	Psalms 93 and 94: The place of faith, and the place of prayer	661
2	Psalms 95 and 96: Tidings of salvation	662
3	Psalms 97 and 98: Visible righteousness	663
4	Psalms 99 and 100: The Lord, holy and good	664

Rev. Eric Alexander, Bible readings

1	Romans 12:1–13	631
2	Romans 12:14–13:14	632
3	Romans 14:1–23	633
4	Romans 15:1–13	634

Other addresses:

Do You Believe in God? by Rev. Michael Baughen	666
Sin: The Breaking of Relationships by Rev. Chris Byworth	667
Failing To Speak to Men by Rev. George Duncan	650
The Second Time by Rev. Eric Alexander	652

The Finished Work of Christ 669
by Rev. Alec Motyer
Lift up Your Eyes 637
by Rev. Andrew Dow
Lord of the Crisis 653
by Rev. Andrew MacRae
The Shepherd Psalm 654
by Rev. Keith Weston
Living under Christ's Lordship 671
by Rev. David Jackman
How Fullness Serves 642
by Rev. George Duncan
The Strengthening of His Spirit 674
by Rev. Michael Baughen
The General Missionary Meeting 643
by Oswald Sanders

These tapes can be obtained, together with a full list of Keswick tapes, from:

Anthony C. Gill, Tape Secretary,
Keswick Convention Tape Library,
13 Lismore Road,
Eastbourne,
East Sussex BN21 3BA

Notes

Notes

Notes

Notes